as bright as the sun

by

cynthia schlichting

The most important journey is the one that leads you home

Nothing is known of Bella's life prior to arriving in the shelter. The pieces of Bella's story prior to arriving at Eagles Den Rescue are my fictional account of her life, and any similarity to actual people or circumstances is purely coincidental. Additionally, the names of certain people, places and entities have been changed to protect their privacy.

Edited by Sharon Honeycutt

Cover design by Kelly Pederson

Copyright © 2012 Cynthia Schlichting
All rights reserved.

ISBN-10: 061563589X
EAN-13: 9780615635897

To Noah, Brady, Olivia and Lucy
May your hearts stay kind forever.
I love you.

contents

1

the skinny brown dog

On a warm, muggy night in September, a skinny brown dog slept restlessly in a small cage on a concrete floor. The only other thing in the cage was a bowl that occasionally contained food but was now dirty and empty. Around the skinny dog's cage were other cages and kennels holding other dogs, and they made lots of noise—but not more than she was accustomed to—so she slept. Her fitful dreams were interrupted when she woke to a man staring at her through the bars of her cage.

His was a face she recognized well, and one that scared her immensely because she saw this man on only two occasions: when she received a little bit of food that made her belly so happy or when something far more sinister was about to happen. She hadn't eaten in what seemed like a very long time, and the last few times the kibble hurt her mouth tremendously. But a small meal that caused her pain was always the more favorable reason for seeing this man, so she sniffed the air hoping for a hint of a tasty snack. The man hadn't brought her something to put in her empty stomach, though, and she could tell immediately that something was different.

For as long as she could remember, the skinny brown dog had been experiencing horrors at the hands of this man, and she had taught herself early on that the best thing to do was hide deep within herself when something bad was about to happen. And that night, she could tell something very bad was about to happen.

The man flung open her cage and grabbed her by the rope that he used as her collar. She couldn't help herself and peed just a little bit. He pulled her to the floor and examined her closely. He pried open her mouth and appeared satisfied. Her mouth hurt so much. She didn't understand why that made him happy, but then the skinny dog never understood why this man did the things he did. When the man grabbed pieces of rope very similar to the rope around her neck, the skinny dog went numb. He tied her front legs together, and he tied her back legs together, and the skinny dog didn't cry or plead. Her eyes simply went blank.

Tonight's auction was very important to the man. He had a dog that he had been grooming and training for a while, and some pretty big-time folks would be there. If this dog performed well enough, it could be a bigger payout than he had seen in a long time.

He'd been out of work for the better part of four years. He was never much of a gambler, but his unemployment checks weren't putting food on the table. His cousin had been a dogman for years and had a pretty impressive collection of fighters—one or two of them his cousin had bought, but most he had bred. He even had a champion.

A champion was a dog that had won three consecutive fights. If the dog went on to win two more, he was considered a grand champion, and a grand champion could go for $10,000 if not more. The man had been doing this for a few years and was lucky enough to have bred a few gems of his own, but most of the pups from his breeding dogs were useless. This dog, though, there was something he liked about this dog. But he needed to be patient and take it one step at a time. If this dog had what the man thought he had, well then, payday was finally coming.

He had to make sure nothing could go wrong, so the man took a very sharp knife and cut deeply through the skinny dog's brown coat into her leg muscle. Seeing blood from the skinny dog before the fight even began would excite and motivate the prize dog and could enhance his performance greatly.

The skinny dog was always so quiet, but the shock of the cut was enough to make her scream in pain. She felt a blow to her face, and then she went quiet again. She could hear the dogs in the pit barking and crying, and she could hear people laughing and cheering. She had heard all of this before, but she could tell that something was different. And as she was thrown into the pit for what could have been the millionth time, she knew what was different. She knew that finally, mercifully, this life was over.

2

brian and cindy

I met Brian in the summer of '96. We had both started new jobs within days of each other at a downtown Minneapolis restaurant popular for lunch and happy hour. Brian was sweet, funny, smart, treated people decently, and was appropriately dedicated to hygiene, so, in other words, not my type at all. But he made me laugh, and he made me think, and we became friends very quickly.

Our friendship spanned the next year and a half or so. Brian had hinted off and on during that time that he was interested in being more than friends, but he had become one of my favorite people. I valued him immensely, and the thought of initiating a relationship and ruining our friendship wasn't something I could bear. So friends we remained.

During this time, we both traveled quite extensively, which is what working in a restaurant in your twenties allows you to do. One of the places that I visited that particularly struck a chord with me was Prague in the Czech Republic. It was beautiful and majestic, and I knew that one day I wanted to live there. When I arrived home from that trip, I immediately applied to a TEFL (Teaching English as a Foreign Language) course. I knew from my research that English teachers were desperately needed in this former Soviet Republic, and I was more than ready to pack up and try something totally new.

Fast forward to a day in April 1998. I was sitting at a stoplight off of I-94 in St. Paul on my way to said TEFL course. A song came on and all of a sudden I was crying. I remember what that song was, what the day was like, the time, everything. A thought came into my head so clearly it was almost like someone whispered it. I have no idea how this happened because the day didn't start out differently than any other. But that moment of clarity gave me this thought, "If you don't marry him, someday you'll wake up and realize another woman is married to your husband." From then on, our friendship was never the same.

At the end of April that same year, Brian and I went out with some friends from work after a shift. Brian and I lagged behind, and I finally got up the courage to say, "Can you come over? I just want to talk to you about something." All he said was, "Here we go."

We made our way back to my shabby, Loring Park apartment near downtown Minneapolis and sat on my retro 1970s couch—retro in a Salvation Army sort of way, not a hip, boutique sort of way. I stammered through something to the effect of, "You were right—I was wrong. I'm so sorry. Maybe we should consider starting a relationship."

With that, Brian dropped an F bomb on me and left, and I'm pretty sure I never respected him more. I now understand that he felt slighted and devalued and that I hadn't done my part to make sure that he understood my feelings were real. But luckily for me, he overlooked my shortcomings, and two days later we were dating. Six months later we were married.

Our married life was unconventional by very general standards right from the start. We weren't out saving lives or changing the world, but we knew we didn't want children, and I was still convinced that Prague was the place for us. Brian was done with school and had taken the "before I join the real world" pre-requisite backpacking trip around Europe with three of his friends. I had persuaded him to visit Prague on the off-chance that he would love it as much as I did and perhaps agree with me that we were just jet-set enough to make an international move.

Brian liked Prague, but he didn't love Prague. He did love me though, so we sold what we could of our belongings and left the rest next to the dumpster by my sad, little apartment. By morning everything was gone, so we figured the decision had been made for us. We had no choice but to move to the Czech Republic. This all seems easy enough when you're two people with no belongings to your names, but there was a catch—actually, there were two catches. And their names were Sadie and Tyra.

Sadie and Tyra were my seven-year-old cats that I had gotten when I was twenty-one. Sadie was a barn cat, and Tyra was a stray that my boyfriend-at-the-time's roommate's flaky girlfriend had brought home. (Got all that?) Well, the flaky girlfriend and the roommate broke up, both moved out, and Tyra stayed. There was never any talk of what they thought would happen to Tyra. I guess they assumed that she would become my responsibility, so my responsibility she became. She and Sadie were best friends and absolutely the loves of my life.

Before Brian, I didn't have much interest in dating, and by my mid-twenties I was kind of over the whole "going out" thing. So, I spent weekends with my girls, cuddled up on the couch, eating take out Thai food from the restaurant across the street, watching The X-Files and

VHS movies, and feeling completely satisfied with my life. When Brian and I decided to move abroad, there was never any question as to whether Sadie and Tyra would come with us. Whether Brian felt the same way, or simply understood my convictions I'm not sure, but I am sure that this staunchly devoted dog-person melted in the presence of the girls—particularly Sadie.

When Brian and I started dating, I think Sadie knew he was the real deal because she hated him immediately. She knew the dates I'd had in the past weren't going to go the distance. Either the guy didn't like me, or I didn't like the guy, but regardless, they always loved Sadie. She was always there to rub legs, sit on laps, or wash her face in the adorable way that cats do. With Brian, not only would she reserve the longest butt-cleaning sessions exclusively for him, but despite his best efforts—chin-rub attempts and numerous tuna offerings—the reception remained icy at best. That is until the day I came home from work and found Brian sitting on the living room floor next to Sadie.

Sadie was on her back, paws in the air ready to strike. Brian would poke her left side, and Sadie would swing to her left side. Brian would poke her right side, and Sadie would swing to her right side. This went on for at least five minutes, and neither one of them had ever looked sweeter or dumber. Their friendship was etched in stone from that moment on. Tyra, on the other hand, could be found anywhere we weren't; she was a much harder sell than Sadie and preferred to give the world the cold shoulder. A full food dish and warm bed equaled love to her. If you found Sadie though, she was probably gazing at Brian like he was the most handsome thing she'd ever seen.

Moving two cats to the Czech Republic isn't easy. If you're thinking about doing it, don't call me—I don't ever want to do it again. I can't remember how many federal government agencies, Czech agencies, and American and foreign veterinarians I talked to, not to mention all the paperwork I completed. But they were my girls, so I didn't begrudge them a second of it. They depended on me, I depended on them, and they were going. With his huge heart, Brian understood this, which meant the world to me.

Our life in the Czech Republic began in March of 1999. Brian and I left in February and travelled around for a month, spending the bulk of our money, assuming that we'd be working and making more once we arrived in Prague. In hindsight, that assumption was adorably naive.

Once Brian and I were settled in the former-Communist, block-style, concrete, one-room flat we'd found, Sadie and Tyra arrived. Life in the Czech Republic was much different than visiting the Czech Republic, but despite feeling like a family of fish out of water, we settled in to life in Prague. Both Brian and I taught English to adult learners and became as fully immersed in the culture as we could. Expenses were higher than expected, and trust me when I say that no one gets rich teaching English. It was a humbling experience thinking of all those American dollars we had wasted en route to Prague, but it taught us the power of a buck and how to live very frugally. Many of the lessons we were forced to learn then are still utilized in our lives today. If a paycheck isn't going to go as far one month because of vet bills, house issues, or whatever, a big pot of beans and rice can last you the better part of a week for less than five dollars. A little tip from me to you.

After spending nearly a year in Prague, we began to think about returning home. Brian was eager to pursue a career in finance. As great as teaching was, he was ready to start utilizing his degree. I had turned thirty while we were in Prague, and while I didn't have the career aspirations that Brian did, I knew unless we wanted to start talking about things like buying a car, finding jobs with better incomes, and getting a bigger flat, there probably wasn't much of a future for us in Prague. Plus, we were eager to see friends and family because not many people had made the trek to visit.

So, a little over a year after we arrived in Prague, we sat at dinner with some of our Czech and American friends, waiting for the bus that would take us to Frankfurt, Germany, and our flight home. (We were too poor to fly out of Prague, so we had to endure a twelve-hour bus ride that included an extensive search of the entire bus at the German border at 2 a.m. We really regretted spending all those dollars.) Sadie and Tyra had been placed on their flight from Prague that afternoon and would arrive back in Minneapolis about an hour before we were scheduled to land, so the timing worked out perfectly. After a very bittersweet good-bye to friends and a country that we had grown unbelievably fond of, we boarded the bus and made our way to Germany. We both stayed awake until we had passed over the border of the Czech

Republic for the last time. We exchanged a look, and I know how heavy Brian's heartfelt because mine felt the same way. When I think back to our time in Prague, it truly was a life-changing experience, and while not all moments were perfect, somehow they all left perfect memories. We slept, and roughly twenty-four hours later we were back in Minneapolis.

Our homecoming was rather unceremonious. We didn't know what to expect, but when you've been away from home for the greater part of a year, you assume that those who love you felt the absence as deeply as you felt it yourself. What we didn't understand was that life goes on whether you're present in it or not. Don't get me wrong—our friends and family were happy to see us and excited we were home, but they would never understand what it's like to feel completely independent and isolated from everything you've ever known. I can only imagine how our soldiers feel, but that's a subject that deserves a book of its own.

I started serving again, which was definitely in my comfort zone. Brian bartended for a while but eventually escaped and got a job as a case manager for an independent financial planning company. But where did that leave me? Brian always had focus and drive and a sense of where he wanted his life to go. I, on the other hand, lacked focus and drive and a sense of where I wanted my life to go. That is until one night in 2002.

Brian and I had gone out with some friends, and I was sitting at the bar trying to get the bartender's attention when I noticed a TV behind the counter. It was playing some Animal Planet show, and while I couldn't hear the dialogue, it kept showing people and dogs running, and then there was a horse, and gradually I stopped worrying about my next cocktail. I started thinking maybe this little Animal Planet show was trying to tell me something—like maybe it was time to go back and finish my degree. Maybe get a degree in, say, biology? With a biology degree I could go on to veterinary school and live my dream life, saving animals' lives. I was just drunk enough for this all to make perfect sense, and within a few weeks I had enrolled for the fall semester at a local university to obtain my biology degree.

Now, if you lack focus and drive, I can tell you that pursuing a degree as challenging as biology may not be the best idea. I've never been a great student, and I can assure you that if my professors remember me at all, it isn't for my brilliant, scientific mind. One thing I do pride myself on though is my commitment to finishing what I start. It's a quality that always surprises me when it rears its unwanted head, but there it was, saying, "This is yet another ugly bed you made." So I laid on it.

While I was in school, Brian worked his way up in the firm and decided it was time for home ownership. Not shockingly, I would have been happy to rent our little apartment with the tiny balcony and very obstructed view of trendy Lake Calhoun forever, but as always, Brian wanted more. We found a fantastic realtor and began our search for the next chapter. We started our hunt focusing on three areas: South Minneapolis, Northeast Minneapolis, and the suburb of St. Louis Park. Shortly into our search, however, it became apparent that our hearts were in Northeast.

Northeast Minneapolis was undergoing a revival. With a mixture of Polish immigrants and young professionals, there are more bars and more churches per square mile in Northeast than anywhere else in the country, at least that's what everyone who lives there says. One of the charms of the area is that you can walk into an old neighborhood bar that smells like stale beer, onion rings, and mildew, get the stare-down from a group of beat-up looking regulars, and find a seat in a "booth" that used to be a church pew. After enjoying a cheap Grainbelt on tap, you can walk right next door to a posh cafe that serves organic eats from sustainable farms. The regulars still stare at you, but this time it's because they're sizing up your shoes. We felt right at home—now we just needed a home.

We looked at several houses in the area and found a beautiful one that we loved, but our much-trusted realtor, Sherri, hated it. In hindsight, the fact that walking around the upstairs gave us vertigo tells us that our realtor was on to something, but the house had all the bells and whistles, and we wanted it. Sherri was unwaveringly opposed to us making this purchase and was busy making phone calls to get us alternate showings while we debated what kind of rug would look best in the living room. She interrupted our decorating plans and said she'd gotten permission for a short-notice showing about a quarter of a mile away. We looked at her map and weren't crazy about the area, but she begged us to look, so we went.

I have a saying that spouses and houses happen for a reason, mainly because of my spouse and my house. When we drove up to the postwar, one-and-a-half story house on the adorable, tree-lined street, we weren't sure what to expect. But when Sherri let us in the front door, we couldn't believe our eyes: a big, beautiful, tiled kitchen; gorgeous hardwood floors in the living room; plenty of natural sunlight; and absolutely zero vertigo. We were home. We packed up our very last apartment and moved into our house on May 3, 2003. Yes, we were home—for what we estimated would be about the next three to five years.

We had been in our house for about a month when Sadie started acting funny. She was our sensitive girl, so we thought she was having a hard time adjusting to her new environment. We called her vet, who basically told us that same thing—new house, new furniture, new smells, new sounds—all could potentially equal trouble for our little girl. Give her some time and call if she got worse. Well, she got worse.

Her appetite appeared to be waning, and she did this funny thing with her mouth, so we decided she needed a dental. Her vet gave her a dental and did an oral exam, but the results were unremarkable; her teeth weren't the source of her issues. We took her to another vet who wanted to "open her up and poke around." (I'm not kidding.) He said sometimes just doing that was enough to make the animal feel better. How that man had a license to practice veterinary medicine will always be beyond me.

At that time I was working with a woman who loved her pets as much as we loved ours. She told us about her vet—the only person my co-worker would trust with her animals. She said her office was in her home. It didn't smell as clean and shiny as a typical vet's office, and she didn't have all the fancy, modern equipment, but my friend had never found anyone as devoted to her pets as Dr. D. So we were on to vet #3.

I called Dr. D. and explained what had been happening with Sadie, and, not surprisingly, she was mortified by the cavalier attitude of the previous vet. Her exact words were, "Please don't cut that cat open." She did extensive testing on Sadie and started her on a round of steroids and, in our eyes, a miracle happened. Our sweet girl, who had become so thin and withdrawn, got the sparkle back in her eyes. Her coat improved. She cuddled with Tyra and played just like she used to. We even found her sleeping in the sun, which was something she hadn't done since she fell ill. We were over-the-moon happy and rejoiced in every moment.

Then it came time to taper her steroid dose down. Steroids are an incredibly wonderful medication, but they're not something that patients can remain on long-term, at least not at the high dose that Sadie was on. So rather than stopping the dosing cold turkey, the dose is gradually reduced in order to wean the body off of the medication. Sadly, within a day or so, it became apparent that we were losing our Sadie again. It was like holding the best, most beautiful gift I'd ever been given and feeling someone pry it from my grasp. I wanted to fight and struggle and hold on to it until my arms or my heart went numb, whichever came first.

Dr. D. knew it was time to say good-bye to Sadie, but I couldn't do it. I pleaded with her to give us a referral to the University Of Minnesota School Of Veterinary Medicine. They took the most complicated cases, and I thought if anyone could cure Sadie, they could. Dr. D. didn't want to do it, I know she didn't, but I pled my case the best way I knew how, and she unwillingly made the phone call that transferred Sadie's care to the U. At this point, Brian believed we were doing the right thing. In his mind, even if they couldn't cure her, maybe we could get some answers as to what was wrong with our girl and at least keep her as comfortable and happy as possible. We brought Sadie to the U in August of 2003.

The treatment was intense and comprehensive, and with each new test my hope grew, Sadie's will faded, and Brian's devotion to see this through diminished. One of the things that I learned from this experience is that in our relationship there are the Heart and the Brains. The Brains knew it was time to let our girl go, but the Heart was selfish and not ready. Instead, a feeding tube was placed, and I subjected our Sadie to numerous tests and procedures. She had to be given a very specific diet at very specific times through that feeding tube. At one point, my coworkers at the restaurant where I was working asked me how the feeding schedule was going. I remember describing it as "time prohibitive."

Sadie, there's a lot I've said to you, and a lot I will always have to say to you, but just know that you were worth everything and more that we did to try and regain your health. When the vets at the university began to talk about repeating CAT scans, X-rays, and other types of testing that Sadie had already been subjected to, we knew our fight was over. Despite everything we subjected our wonderful girl to, a diagnosis was never made. In the end, it was the outcome I dreaded. Tears are running down my face now as I remember the pain in saying good bye to our dear Sadie. She left this world on September 15, 2003, three short months and a nest egg after becoming ill, held in the rug that she had always liked to sleep on, with Brian and me cradling her, whispering our love to her.

I am not a person that can say I've lived a life of no regrets. I've had regrets—plenty of them. One of those regrets is Sadie. If I live to be 100 years old, I'll never forgive myself for not looking in her eyes and knowing that she was done fighting. In talking to some of my other "crazy-pet" friends, they've said that your pet will always hang on until they know you're ready to let them go. While these words are kind, they make me feel even worse. A sweet, spoiled, gentle, thirteen-year-old, six-pound cat has the strength to fight when she's got no fight left simply because her selfish mother can't stand the thought of living life without her. So Sadie, I tell you this a lot, but here it is again. I'm so sorry for the amount of suffering I put you through. You'll never know how sorry. I know it doesn't help, but it was all because of how desperately I loved you and wanted as much time with my beautiful girl as I could get. I still love and miss you tremendously, and I hope that through you I've learned a valuable lesson in letting go. I love you sweet girl.

Sadie also taught me the value in appreciating the Brains. The nicknames the Brains and the Heart aren't meant to imply that Brian doesn't have a heart—he does, and a big one. And I do have a brain, though it's never going to be a hotly contested debate amongst our friends as to which of us is the sensible one. I call him the Brains because he is able to see things with love and with rationality. That's something I'm not able to do, at least not as well. I'll always wish I had listened to him.

Time trudges on, and when you're mourning someone who never really had a place in your home, it becomes a limbo of sorts. Sadie became sick almost immediately after we purchased and moved into our house, and we never really built up the memories of "this is where she slept in the sun," or, "aww, her bird watching spot," or, "eww, here's where she always puked." Our grieving felt abbreviated and insufficient, and the house that we had fallen in love with seemed a little less personal.

Tyra went through a change as well. She had watched her friend deteriorate over the three-month period of her illness, and now we noticed that flakes dusted her pitch black coat. She would search for long periods of time—under beds, behind the couch, in the basement. She was obviously trying to find her best friend. We could have thought that this was just part of the aging process for Tyra; she was, after all, going on fourteen, but it was quite obvious what was happening. It was about six months after we lost Sadie that Tyra began to bathe herself more regularly, which was good because the cat dandruff was kind of disgusting. Her appetite improved as did her disposition. She had been grieving too much over Sadie to be concerned about hygiene or food. I had read a lot about pets feeling grief, so there was no doubt in my mind that Tyra deeply felt the loss of Sadie. As Tyra seemed to return to normal, our lives seemed to as well. We began to wonder whether it was time to welcome another member to our family. What better way to reward Tyra than to bring a big, new, strange dog into the house?

We began looking at the Humane Society of Hennepin County's website and fell head over heels with a number of the dogs that we saw. We started looking at the website in December 2003, just to get a lay of the land. There was a white dog named something I can't remember, and in my most naïve state I thought, "if she's still there when we're ready to adopt, she's OURS!" Well, that mystery white dog was gone the next day. It wasn't the holding tank that we thought it was. Dogs came in, and most were quickly adopted out, most, but not all. This would be our first dog together and my first dog, period. We knew we would love this dog like crazy, and we knew we'd do everything we could to take the best care of him or her possible. But did we know we were on the way to becoming "crazy dog people?" Nope, but then again we hadn't met Foster.

...

At about this same time, somewhere near the border of North and South Carolina, a mother dog rested underneath the porch of a timeworn white house. The paint on the house was chipping, and if someone walked across that porch, the mother dog was always surprised they didn't fall right through and join her. But she had bigger things than that to worry about: inside of her were babies that were just about ready to greet the world.

The mother dog lay very still and thought about how eager she was to welcome them. She'd had puppies before and was a good mother. She loved everything about them already. She knew how they'd smell, how often they would need to nurse, and how she would give them kisses to bathe those sweet babies in her smell. It was cool underneath the porch and she liked that. The soothing sound of the wind in the trees and grasses lulled her off to sleep.

When she awoke, it was dark out; nighttime had arrived while she was resting. She was feeling anxious and began pacing. She tried to nest and get comfortable, but she simply couldn't and she knew why. Her babies would be here soon. She continued pacing and began panting. The pain began in her belly and continued to get worse and worse the longer she paced. She couldn't help herself and began to whine. She tried to keep herself occupied by adding more dirt to her nest, but that just made her feel worse. She retched and vomited, and still the pain in her belly persisted. She didn't know how long she had felt like this, but the sun was starting to rise, cutting through the misty Carolina fog.

Panting still, she was grateful the porch remained dark and hadn't been warmed yet by the early morning sunshine. She could see slats of light coming through the boards, and she heard someone walk across the porch. They must have heard her too because suddenly there was that little boy's face peeking at her though the trellis. She liked that boy, but she wasn't in the mood for company, and she tried to explain this to him by baring her teeth and growling, just a little. She heard him shout something, and pretty soon it sounded like someone else was falling through that porch. Then the woman's face was looking at her. The woman was fine, but she raised her voice more than the mother dog liked, so she steered clear of the woman most of the time. The woman took the boy by the shoulders and led him away, and the dog was happy about this. She was exhausted and anxious and wanted to be alone with her puppies when the time came.

Suddenly she felt an incredible pain tear through her belly and fluid run down her legs. She was too tired to do anything but lie in the nest that she'd tried to improve during the night. She felt her belly tighten and knew it was time to meet her first puppy. She strained and strained and before too long a tiny, chubby puppy was there. She knew to lick that baby like crazy, which is what she did. She bit the umbilical cord, and, with that, she and her puppy were separated. She was already a good mom. The day went on, and, as the slats of light through those boards got longer and the day got dimmer, she welcomed more and more babies.

It had been dark for a while by the time she welcomed her final puppy, and, in all, without fanfare or celebration, eight little ones came into the world that day. That mama dog was so proud of all her pups, a mother's love doesn't know how to decide which one is more special than the others, because they're all special. But puppy number six was born during that singular twilight hour when anything is possible and everything is imaginable. Puppies should have a happy life, and number six would have a very happy life, to start. But her start would not be her finish, and, thankfully, that amazing mama didn't have any idea what lie in store for her sweet number six.

3

foster

Tyra, Brian, and I welcomed 2004 without much to-do. Brian and I hadn't gone out to celebrate New Year's Eve since we lived in Prague, and that was fine with us. Dinner at home, a little champagne (or maybe a lot), and watching people freeze their asses off in Times Square was plenty good enough for us. Tyra had gotten much better. She was bouncing back and becoming our snooty but lovable girl again. So like we said, what would be a better prize for her than a brand-spanking new dog?

We were still checking the humane society's website, and as I said before, dogs came and went. There was one dog, though, whose face remained on the site. He was a goofy-looking guy with a really long tongue named Buddy. Buddy was a German Shepherd/Rottweiler mix. I can't remember what his link said about him, other than he had been with his previous owners for four years, and they couldn't keep him because they were being relocated. He was cute, for sure, but not necessarily cuter than any of the others dogs—plus, we weren't ready just yet. Over the next couple of months, I would guess we checked the site about three to four times per week, and, inevitably, a dog that we were interested in was gone. Buddy wasn't though. As time marched on and Buddy didn't, I began to suspect that this was the pup that would be coming home with us when adoption day came.

One day, Brian and I decided to get serious, and we logged onto the site together. Well, there was Buddy and that tongue, staring at us from the home page of the humane society's website, and Buddy had been named the "Shelter Star." I had brought up Buddy in the past, but Brian wasn't sold. He was unsure why Buddy had been there almost three months; he was unsure of how Tyra would react to a bigger, older dog; he was unsure how a bigger, older dog would react to Tyra. As Brian was walking out of our home office at the end of our dog-shopping session, I said to him, "You know it's gonna be you, me, and Buddy walking out of that place." Brian said nothing. That could have been a good or a bad sign; he's perfected the art of the "definite maybe."

The beginning of March 2004 was blustery, which isn't uncommon in Minnesota. Brian had taken Wednesday, March 3, off, and we had christened it "D-Day" (Dog Day, we're not that clever). On March 2, we sat in a fetid, hard rock-focused bar that was not even close to our house. (I have no idea how we ended up there.) We talked anxiously and excitedly about who would be joining our family.

If we adopted a girl, we knew we wanted to name her "Mirka," which was a very popular female name in the Czech Republic and one that we both thought was beautiful. But what if we brought home a boy? We had no idea what we would name a male. I still wasn't holding out a lot of hope for Buddy, though I thought we'd be the perfect family for him. Brian had a lot more experience with dogs than I did, and he was probably right that a large, mixed-breed dog might be too much for an inexperienced, first-time dog owner like me—plus, there was always Tyra to consider. We sat and speculated and watched children run around the bar shockingly unattended and then both of us saw it at the same time—the florescent "Fosters" beer sign. We were beside ourselves! It was the perfect name found in the perfect way for us. So, if the doggy-stork delivered a boy, then Foster it was.

We got home that night and tried to prepare for a visitor that we hadn't yet met and who would stay forever. This adoption was a strange and wonderful thing. This was the only one where we had no idea what we were getting going in. We weren't crazy dog people yet. Were we getting a big dog, a small dog, a special needs dog? We had no idea. We just knew we needed the dog that needed us. That day before D-Day we bought the bed, the dog dishes, the toys, and the collar and leash. We put away anything and everything that a new dog could possibly break. We secured the garbage cans and baby-locked the cabinets. We were ready.

That morning when we woke up, we didn't say much, and I'm wondering if I asked Brian now if he'd remember how we felt and interacted that morning. There was a definite uncertainty between us, and I know we were questioning whether this was the right decision. We kissed Tyra and assured her that everything would be OK. She looked at us like she wasn't convinced, but that's how she always looked at us. We did a last-minute surveillance of our house and realized that looking at it through a different set of eyes made our house look like a different house, and in many ways, it would be a different house. We would be a family of four again, and I decided I couldn't wait.

Anyone who has ever gone through the process of adopting a dog through a shelter knows how trying it is. As joyful as the experience is, there is an enormous amount of heartbreak seeing all those hopeful faces come to the front of their pens, just begging for a pat on the head and a chance to tell you their stories. And each dog's eyes definitely told a story.

Sure enough, as we were walking into the kennel area, there was a sign at the entrance with Buddy's picture and his coveted "Shelter Star" status. Not only was there a deep discount on this dog, but they were also throwing in a kennel, food, some toys—basically the works. This dog wasn't just on sale, he was on clearance.

As we walked between the rows of kennels, any dog that didn't have someone already standing at its kennel contemplating an adoption would run forward and yap, tail and tongue wagging. It was impossible not to fall in love with each and every one. We took our time with each, and as we made our way down, I could feel myself becoming more and more apprehensive until finally, we were one kennel away from Buddy's. No one was standing there, and I couldn't see Buddy from where we were. We took our time with Buddy's next-door neighbor and then moved on. OK, the moment of truth. There he was.

There was no joy in seeing Buddy for the first time. What we saw was an incredibly thin dog who looked as dejected as anyone I've ever seen. His frail frame revealed his fast, shallow breathing. The toys that the staff had so graciously placed there for him looked untouched. The shelter staff had also placed rugs and a second kennel inside his larger one. I'm guessing they had put the smaller kennel in so that Buddy could seek solace from the barking and whining he had been subjected to for the last close-to-four months. Bless their hearts; they had done their best to make this a good temporary home for Buddy.

Buddy was lying on one of those rugs facing the opposite direction, so in my happiest voice I started calling his name, but Buddy didn't respond. Brian tried to woo him as well but achieved the same outcome. A shelter volunteer saw us taking some time at Buddy's kennel and came rushing over. I can't remember her name, but I remember she had an accent—Australian, I think. I remember that she had two big dogs of her own, and she started telling us all about how to kennel train. She was very, very sweet. The sight of her had even somewhat snapped Buddy out of his funk, and he came to get some attention.

She then moved the conversation delicately to him. She was in love with that dog, and she said she prayed every time that she showed up for a volunteer shift that Buddy would have gone home, but he was always there. She said he was a lovely and resilient spirit who just needed a secure place with people who had patience and a willingness to work with a dog that definitely had issues but that was worth the commitment. In describing what life with Buddy would probably be like, her honesty sadly sealed his fate. We could see the sorrow on her face as we told her that we were inexperienced dog owners. We weren't equipped to handle an insecure or unpredictable dog, and bringing him into our home would probably be a disservice to us all. With a very heavy heart, we moved onto the next kennel.

Somewhere down the line we came to another dog. An overweight, white lab mix named, you guessed it, Buddy. This dog was a couple of years old and ready to embrace life in a new home. He was exuberant and eager to go out into the introduction run and spend some time with us. His weight would be something that we would need to manage, especially as he grew older, but other than that, for all practical purposes, this dog was perfect.

We tossed the ball and talked it over, and I once again brought up Buddy #1. Brian went over the same insecurities as he had before, and I knew he was right. Ironically, we'd be taking Buddy home after all. We made our way inside to start the paperwork while Buddy #2 made his way back to his kennel, which now had the sought-after "Hold" sign on it. As we approached the front desk, the staff must have gotten wind of our interest in Buddy #1 because one of them said very excitedly as we approached, "Is Buddy going home today?" The staff member that was working with us said quietly, "The other Buddy." Three faces behind that desk fell, and one of the women handed us the paperwork that would make the adoption final.

We were about halfway through the application when I began looking at Brian. Now, if you ask my parents, they'll tell you that I've been a champion pouter ever since I popped out of the womb, and I must have been delivering some really good stuff because Brian looked at me and said, "What do you want to do?"

I said, "Can we just take one more look?" OK, The Brains could have said anything that would have re-convinced the Heart that it wasn't a good idea. He could have reminded me that we had a fourteen-year-old cat and that we had no experience. What if Buddy became aggressive, what if we didn't know how to discipline him, what if our fence wasn't tall enough for such a big dog? He could have said any of those things, but the Brains said simply, "Yes."

We walked back up to the front desk and asked the first woman we saw if we could take one more look at Buddy (#1). It was as if we'd told a six-year-old that from now on, every day would be either Christmas or her birthday. She got on the phone immediately, and, in under a minute, another staff member was by our side, whisking us back to Buddy #1's kennel.

When we got there, another couple was standing in front of us, so we took a step back and waited our turn. They were trying the same tactics Brian and I had tried to get the Shelter Star to come to the front of the kennel and make an appearance, but Buddy wasn't interested. You could tell he had given up, and it was heartbreaking. What happened next still angers me enough to make the back of my neck get hot. The woman turned to the man, laughed, and said, "He must be feeling the rejection." Then they walked away.

My first instinct was to give her a solid groin punch, but in hindsight I suppose what I owed her was thanks. Her insensitivity and general poor taste in humor shifted our focus, which became immediately and solely on Buddy #1. This guy needed us, and we needed him. Maybe we were the perfect match. Maybe we'd get him home, and he would take a look around and settle in immediately. Maybe he and Tyra would be best friends right out of the gate, and we'd be watching them snuggle in a matter of hours. Maybe the fence was actually taller than we remembered ... maybe. And just like that, the Brains agreed that Buddy was coming home.

The available sign went back on Buddy #2's kennel, and we went up to give the three faces the news. It was one moment in our lives that we felt very important. I'm pretty sure that every available staff member came to meet us and tell us every Buddy story they had. This was his steak toy that he loved. He was sort of ball-obsessive, but if you know him, it's actually cute. He's gassy right now, but once you get him home that should settle down. Their exuberance was contagious and helped convince us we were making the right decision. They took us down the aisles of the humane society and picked out the things they thought would help Buddy thrive in his new home. This dog really was on clearance. Then the shelter director was there when we were ready to walk out the door with Buddy #1.

She explained to us that Buddy was a dog that had issues when he came into the shelter. She explained that the months he had been there had been difficult for him, and then she said six words that made us realize it was meant to be. She said, "He'll be like a foster child." There it was; he'll be like a foster child indeed, our Foster. She also said, "Don't worry. Buddy (#2) will be gone tomorrow." When we checked the humane society's website the next day, we discovered she was right. What had taken Foster months to achieve, this dog had done in a matter of days. Buddy #2 had gone home.

Bringing Foster home was both much easier and more difficult than we expected. Our puppy-proofing seemed silly because Foster was older and not really interested in causing any real discontent. He was, however, very nervous about his new environment and paced incessantly. He paced before he ate and after he ate and before he went outside and while he was outside and after he came inside from outside. It seemed as though he had worked a track into our hardwood floors. I had never lived with a dog before, and Brian just had his family dog growing up, so there came that "inexperienced dog owner" thing again. Were we doing ok by Foster? Was this level of anxiety normal for a dog recently adopted? We obviously had no idea what we were doing, so we just did our best to keep Foster happy, calm, and comfortable.

While we were at one of his initial vet visits, a friendly woman holding a cat was seated next to us. She commented on Foster's protruding bones, and we self-consciously explained his months in the shelter and the toll it had taken on him. She was understanding and told us how she had also adopted a special needs dog. She told us about her experience, and then she said something that made my blood run cold. She said, "You need to give it about two years." You've got to be kidding me.

We made our way into the vet's office and watched Foster get inspected. His ears looked good, and through a quick inspection of his teeth, the vet agreed that four years old was probably about right. But his coat was dull, he was shedding profusely, and he was grossly underweight. Foster weighed forty-nine pounds at that vet visit, and his vet determined that a healthy weight for him would be between seventy-five and eighty pounds. We had a long ways to go, and the constant pacing wasn't going to help. On a scale of one to five, with five being the worst, she gave his appearance a four-and-a-half but said he had "good bones." Help him settle in and get him to gain some weight and you should have a great dog. Sounds easy, right?

Well, the first months of our relationship with Foster were interesting to say the least. The pacing continued, which may not seem like such a big deal, but it was surprisingly exhausting. He would pace in circles or from room to room for literally two to three hours at a time. Then, if we were lucky, he would settle down for a quick nap. But then what would usually happen is someone would make a noise in the kitchen, or he'd hear the toilet flush, or the phone would ring two doors down, or a leaf would fall off of a tree outside and he would be off of the couch, pacing again. We tried so hard not to get frustrated with him, but sometimes it was enough to keep everyone on edge. He drove Tyra insane, and she would either take a jab at him or shoot us a nasty "screw you" look before heading for higher ground.

We walked him as frequently as we could, to try and work off some of this nervous energy, but this wasn't always the relaxing family activity it should have been either. On Foster's info sheet at the shelter, they had given him a "good" rating regarding leash behavior. What I'll say about that is they either flat-out lied, or Foster conveniently forgot all that good leash behavior once he came home with us. I've never seen a dog more inept on a leash; it was as though he'd never been exposed to a walk in his life. He would attempt to make these enormous circles while walking, which meant we had to stop every half block or so to untangle ourselves from him. If we tried to hold the leash tightly so as not to give him much leeway, we simply got dragged in whatever direction he decided to go. It was amazing to me that a dog that thin had that much strength. Our walks were an absolute embarrassment, and if I had a dollar for each time a neighbor asked who was walking whom, I'd have about seventeen dollars. This dog, and more importantly Brian and I, needed some training.

We signed up for training classes at one of the popular pet store chains. Again, knowing little to nothing about having a dog—let alone training one—this seemed like a perfectly acceptable idea. Class was on Monday and Wednesday nights, and when we showed up that first night, we found out it was just Foster and an adorable little four-month old puppy in the class. "Great!" we thought. "Foster will be able to get all kinds of one-on-one attention!" In actuality, red flags should have been going off all over the place.

This adorable, little four-month old puppy stole the limelight and our trainer's heart. She fawned and cooed over the pup, giving our rag-tag dog and pony show (minus the pony) the short end of the session. The trainer appeared visibly frustrated by our four-year-old, forty-nine-pounder. Don't get me wrong, Foster had shown up in all his glory. He was pacing, restless, and completely unfocused. To make matters worse, he had come across a tennis ball that became the center of his universe; nothing she could do or offer him would convince him that giving up that tennis ball was a good idea. So that became the focus of the whole session—coaxing Foster to part with his new best friend. Suffice it to say that monumental progress was not made with our dog that night.

While we understood our instructor's exasperation, we also understood that she was a certified dog trainer, and we doubted that Foster was the worst case she'd ever seen. She did at one point say working with him was "like trying to get a child with ADD to do math while he's watching fireworks at the state fair." Huh, so maybe he was the worst she'd ever seen.

What we had hoped would be a positive bonding experience between us and Foster turned into a disaster. We left feeling dejected and frustrated with ourselves and with poor ADD-at-the-state-fair Foster. When we got home, he was still visibly agitated and anxious, so I thought taking him for a walk would be a good idea. We started out as night fell, and it was nothing surprising: circles, pulling, tangles, and tripping. I thought to myself, "Maybe running would feel good to him!" We started off at a decent clip, and I was proud of myself for coming up with something that might actually calm our guy down until we heard a diabolical hissing sound and ran right into the crosshairs of a neighbor's cat. The cat leapt out of the darkness and attacked our dog unpityingly and resolutely until I could pry him off of Foster's hind quarters. It just wasn't Foster's day.

We tried a different, more specialized training program that produced similar results, and in the end we decided that maybe all this structure and discipline wasn't for us. Yes, he was restless and anxious at times; yes, he continued to pace; and yes, he maintained a spot in his heart and soul reserved exclusively for tennis balls. (Once he got a taste for them, there was no going back.) But he didn't jump on the counters, he came when called, and he didn't tear up the house or the yard, so why put him through all of these additional stressors? On that note, why put us through them either? We didn't need someone telling us how rotten our dog was, when in reality it was just as we had believed it was the day we took him home from the shelter. He needed us and we needed him, and he was perfect.

Turns out the unofficial two-year rule proved to be accurate, and after so many months of our bargaining, pleading, and peaceful-music-playing, Foster decided in 2006 that pacing was over-rated. To our dismay, the pacing was then replaced with "guard-dogging," which we soon discovered was equally exhausting. If a person approached the house, especially someone ballsy like the mailman, Foster would go absolutely insane, spinning and barking and snarling irrationally at the window. Never mind that the mail had been delivered every day since we bought the place without incident, Foster was pretty sure that mailman was up to no good. Every morning at about 11 a.m., Foster would stand vigil in hopes that this would be the day when the mailman got the untimely demise he had coming. Every day he gives his most fearsome performance, but after more than six years, I'm very happy to report the mail is still uneventfully being delivered, and Foster is still convinced that guy is not on the up and up.

In the meantime, Foster and Tyra developed the definitive "love-hate" relationship. Foster loved Tyra and Tyra hated Foster. Foster would do his absolute best to sneak in a butt sniff whenever possible, which infuriated Tyra. Foster would always be aware of where Tyra was, whether it was the kitchen, bathroom, guest room, or wherever. He somehow knew when she had stood up to find a better place to nap, and he'd sneak behind her while she was making her move. She became stealth-like in her abilities to pretend she didn't see the impending sniff coming, and would then launch a formidable counter-strike that would always land squarely on Foster's nose. The pain and shame were never a deterrent though, and his attempts continued.

Being the mixed breed that he was, you wouldn't think that Foster would be very friendly with cats. A German Shepherd/Rottweiler mix sounds ferocious and not at all cat-friendly, let alone anything-friendly.

But what the media has told you about these breeds is often-to-always deceiving, at the expense of these wonderful dogs. Foster, with all of his quirks and shortcomings, was really an amazingly friendly dog. He loved Tyra without fault and loved Brian and me conditionally. That's right, conditionally. If he was in the right mood and we hadn't done anything to make him mad in the last forty-eight hours, he might come around for a tummy rub. Otherwise, forget it. That being said, he was a sweet and wise soul, and he relied on our affection more than he wanted to admit. And because of him we became interested in both aspects of his breed.

My brother-in-law Jim had a pit bull named Doo when I was in my 20s, and that dog was one of the sweetest souls I've met to date. He was chummy and hammy and soft to the touch, and I loved him dearly. Doo got me interested in "problem breeds" early on. Foster's part-Rott-weiler-ness had gotten Brian and I even further interested in these mis-understood dogs—breeds that, in the hands of the right owner, want simply to love and be loved; that have been persecuted and damned in the eyes of society; that are abused and vilified and neglected and overbred. These breeds were the ones that Brian and I became pas-sionate about, and soon a Rottweiler named Jane would enter our lives.

4

puppy number 6

The mama dog would remember her puppies as squealing and happy. One by one, they were scrutinized by potential families for their willingness to fish, hunt, cuddle, or whatever else the family would require of him or her. They were a roly-poly pile of feet, fur, and noses. Every morning the boy looked through the trellis at those puppies and dreaded the day that he would have to say good-bye to them all. It wasn't the first litter of puppies this mama had had, and it probably wouldn't be the last, but oh, how the boy wished he could keep just one of those little wigglers for himself. But it seemed each day another puppy was whisked away to whatever fate had in store for it.

Some would be lap dogs, some would help their master with hunting or guarding, and that would be the extent of their relationship. Most would have at least reasonably happy lives, and that's what their mama wanted for them—a family that would love those babies almost as much as she did. That was the only thing in the world that truly mattered to her. Yes, she liked to stay warm or stay cool, she loved a full belly, and she loved a good scratch on the head every now and then, but she would give all that up if it meant her babies' lives would be filled with even more warmth, comfort, full bellies, and head scratches than she had ever known.

The first half of the puppies had already been adopted out when a family pulled up in a noisy, green, four-door pickup. It rumbled up the driveway and stopped about twenty feet from where Mama was sleeping with her puppies. She peeked out from underneath the trellis, and from the way two girls bounded out of the back seats, she could tell they had come for one of her babies. A familiar feeling swept over her. She was sad, yes, and she would miss them immensely, but they were getting bigger. As much as she loved them, they were becoming somewhat of a nuisance with their continuous crying to nurse from her. She knew it was time for them to begin their own lives with their own families. She looked around at what was left of her sleeping brood and wondered which one would be getting in that big, noisy pickup and leaving her forever.

Her liquid brown eyes peeked at the family again. This time all four were out of the truck and were making their way to the house. The man was tall and wasn't saying much. The woman also seemed soft-spoken, which the mama liked; the woman that Mama lived with raised her voice so much, and she didn't like that. She did like the way those little girls made her feel, though. They had so much energy, and the way they ran up to the house told the mama just how excited they were to be bringing one of her babies home. She could hear them stomping across that old rickety porch, and pretty soon there were five faces staring at her from the trellis.

The woman who raised her voice too much reached her arm in and, one by one, grabbed a puppy. As she did this, the mama decided she'd go out and give this family the once-over. By the time she made it outside, those two girls were cooing and kissing one of her puppies, and she knew which one it was. It was her sweet number six. She knew this because when her number six was happy, she didn't just wag her tail, she got her whole backside in on the act, and sure enough, this puppy's whole back half was shaking back and forth as if meeting this family was the greatest thing that ever happened to her. And with that, Mama was happy. Her number six had a family, and it was a good one. She was sure of it.

•••

It was hard to imagine leaving the familiar, musty smell beneath her porch, but puppy number six had no choice as she was carried by a bouncy, excited, shrill little girl. She looked over the little girl's shoulder and watched her porch, her siblings, and—most importantly—her mother get farther and farther away. She wasn't sure how she should feel, so she felt sad. She could tell that this little girl would love her, and she wanted her heart to feel free and love her right back. And she would, it would just take a little while.

They reached the truck, and the family that now numbered five got into the noisy, four-door pickup and made their way back down the driveway. Again, puppy number six was being held in such a way that she could peek over the girl's shoulder and watch her home fade into the distance. In her heart she knew she'd never again smell the stale leaves and earth that made up her home. She knew she'd never pile up with her siblings while they raced to nurse from her mama all at once.

At the minute of her deepest concern, the man turned on music that filled the cabin, and puppy number six must have liked it because her tail started wagging. She looked around the pick-up, and the two girls and the woman were looking at her. They chatted and carried on with her and each other, and puppy number six got very excited. The looks on their faces were new to her, and they made her feel good. Her mama had made her feel like heaven, but she knew her mama loved her, so she expected to feel like that. But these people—they didn't have to look at her with kind eyes.

Amidst their chatter she kept hearing the word "Lexie." They would say that word while looking directly in her eyes. She didn't know what it meant, but they said it with such affection that she quickly grew fond of that word. She realized that she liked them very much, and, after an excited meet-and-greet with each and every member of the family, (which ended with a quick heave-ho into the back seat when she got a little too boisterous with the driver), she let the hum of the motor lull her into a cozy nap right in the little girl's lap—a spot, by the way, that made her much happier than looking over the girl's shoulder.

As the rumble of the motor softened, they slowly rolled to a stop. Number six-now-Lexie woke from her nap and looked out the window. She couldn't see her musty porch, but that didn't surprise her. She could still hear that pleasant music and those faces were just as sweet, so she decided she was on a once-in-a-lifetime adventure. The roll of the engine came to a halt, and the door opened, revealing her new home. She was hesitant to get out of the cabin, so the mother and one of the girls got out and began to coax her. They sounded cheerful and enthusiastic and made kissing noises at her, so she had no choice but to get excited, jump out, and investigate her new surroundings.

Lexie's nose was going like crazy; this place was a little different than where she had come from. There were trees and lots of green grass where she had been, and she really liked that. This place seemed a little harder. Things weren't as forgiving—there were lots of rocks and dirt where she walked, but that wasn't necessarily bad. There were patches of grass where she could relieve herself, and there certainly were interesting smells to scrutinize for hours—she would never get bored. She noticed a pen at one side of the yard. When she checked it out, she found a nice, soft bed inside it as well as a dish that held some pretty tasty food. It seemed like a good enough place for a nap when she was ready, but she wasn't nearly ready yet. She grabbed a quick nibble and continued her survey. While she was exploring, she kept looking to make sure she could tell where all those people were. Sure enough, every time she looked, they were watching her with smiling eyes.

The girls and Lexie played and played and played. Someone brought out a ball, and after several rounds of "pry the ball out of Lexie's mouth so you can throw it again," Lexie realized if she got the ball and then dropped it, this enormously fun game would continue for what seemed like forever. She ran in the sun until her back was sizzling and her throat was dry and hot. The soft-spoken woman brought out some water, and Lexie didn't think that anything had ever tasted better. She drank the cool, crisp water until her belly felt bloated. Then she saw the people sitting at a table in the shade, so she went and lay by the man's feet. She fell asleep to the sweet sounds of ice clinking in glasses, laughing voices, and the wind in her overturned ear.

When Lexie woke, it was starting to get dark out, and the family was gathering all their things and heading towards the house. Lexie looked around, taking a moment to reconnect with her new surroundings. She never felt scared, but she did feel a hole in the pit of her stomach when she realized her mama wasn't here. Then she heard the shrill little girl talking to the man, and she remembered that she thought it was nice here.

Lexie headed toward the house with them, but once they got to the house, the man turned and placed a foot even with Lexie's chest, saying the words that from that point on would cause her sadness. "No, Lexie." The girls kissed her goodnight, and the family walked into the house and closed the door.

All of a sudden the early evening light seemed like total darkness. She looked around the yard where, only hours before, she and the girls had been playing and having the time of their lives. What had seemed so energizing and new now seemed lonely and cold. She sniffed around again hoping to get a whiff of something that would catch her interest and take her mind off of how much she was starting to miss her mama, but she was too preoccupied with how strange her surroundings felt.

All of the noises that she had heard that afternoon seemed different now. They seemed louder and sadder than they had when she was playing in the sunlight. Bugs kept landing on her ears, back, and legs, so she shook to get them off. Every once in a while she'd get a stinging little pain when one of those pests would bite her. She remembered that she had seen the pen with the tasty food on the other side of the yard, and that seemed like it might be a good place for a reprieve, so she made her way back over and examined it again. The bed did look comfortable and the food looked tasty, so she had another nibble and lay down. Her eyes wanted to close and take a nap—she was still exhausted from her day of fun-in-the-sun—but every time she closed them, she saw her mama under that porch.

She tried to smell the damp staleness of her home, but this place smelled different. In her mind she pictured her remaining two brothers and sister underneath the porch with her mama—how they were snuggled close and snoring. Did they miss her? Did they look at each other before they floated off to sleep and wonder where their number six had gone? The night got darker, and she felt more and more isolated. She must have dozed off for a while because when she woke up she felt content and safe. But then she looked around and saw all the dirt and rocks in the yard and remembered that she was nowhere near her porch.

She looked towards the house where she had seen those people go—she didn't know how long ago—and she longed to be inside. She wanted to go and paw at the door, but she was too afraid to leave her little pen. The night was black now, and she didn't like it one bit. She let out a little whimper. Maybe if the family heard her, they would realize that she should be inside with them. She could curl up at the man's feet again, and everyone would feel safe and everyone would feel happy, and in the morning she would show them how happy they had made her by playing the best game of ball that she could. Her little whimper got no response from the family, so she whimpered again, this time a little bit louder. Again, she heard nothing in response.

Lexie was trying to be brave, but she was scared and lonely and frustrated. If these people didn't want her to be with them, why didn't they just leave her with her mama? The last time the night was this dark, she was snuggled with her brothers and her sister in a happy mound and that's exactly where she wanted to be now. She decided to voice her frustrations with a series of loud barks which were met by a harshness that she hadn't heard in the man's voice before and that she didn't ever want to hear again. Her lonely, sad spirit was met with, "Shut up Lexie!" when the man opened the window and yelled at her. She desperately tried to look through the darkness and that window to show the man how sad and lonesome she felt, but she heard the window close and was by herself again in midnight seclusion.

That night and many more like it passed. Lexie grew accustomed to her life in the yard. She loved to see the girls come running to greet her, whether it was in the morning light, the hot afternoon sun, or the twilight of the evening. She loved her games of fetch, and she loved, loved, loved to take rides in that noisy pick-up. The man would walk down the path towards the big, green, grumbly machine, and if she was very lucky, she'd hear, "Let's go, Lexie." Lexie would fly down the path after him and leap into the passenger's side.

She loved everything about how the pick-up ride made her feel including being by the man and having her head out the window. Every once in a while a car would pull up alongside of Lexie in the truck, and she could see them point and chuckle; she knew that they probably had a Lexie of their own that they liked to take for drives. Her favorite part of the drives reminded her of when she first arrived home with her family—when the roar of the engine got lower and lower, and the sound of the gravel became more distinct as they got closer to their destination, until it crunched under their tires as the truck drew to a stop.

The years went on and Lexie settled into her routine with her family. She loved them dearly and would have done anything in her power to protect them and keep them safe. Around the same time every afternoon she would sit by the edge of their yard and wait. And at almost exactly the same time her girls would come walking up the path toward the house. They were still the shrieking, screaming heaps of energy that they had been four years earlier, and though Lexie had slowed down some, she still ran toward them with her mouth open in a wide smile, and her backside wagging.

The girls had grown some but were still very excitable, and as soon as Lexie came into view, they would always run to hug her and tell her about their day. They loved her soft brown coat and thick skin around her neck that, if it got bunched up just so above her collar, became a big, fuzzy brown cowl neck where the girls could bury their faces and forget all their troubles. In addition to her neck roll, she had funny tail rolls to match. No one was quite sure what kind of dog she was, but no one really cared either. The girls had grown up whispering their secrets in her ear, crying tears into that comforting neck roll, and taking naps in the sun on the belly that had produced exactly three litters of puppies. The family tried to keep Lexie safe and contained when she went into heat, but every once in a while a scoundrel made his way onto the property. About two months after each of those visits, squinty, squirmy little bundles of joy would arrive. She had produced sixteen puppies in her life, and she had been just as good of a mama as her mama had been. She hoped somehow her mama knew this and was proud of her.

Lexie was just as excited to see the girls as they were to see her. She knew their voices as well as she knew every thought she had ever had. There was nothing that she wouldn't do for them. She still had times when she would look longingly toward the house and try to will an invitation out of the family, but she never got one. There had been two occasions when she had snuck into the house, and she had relished that! Her family's smells were everywhere. She saw chairs that were much softer than the ones they sat on outside—and the beds! She thought her soft bed outside was good, but the ones that she found in the house were tall and soft, and if she ever got the chance to lie on one of them, she might never leave. Inevitably, someone would catch her inside and shoo her back to the yard. She accepted this, though, and was just happy to have the time to listen to secrets, soak up tears, and be a willing pillow for her sweet girls.

That evening when they sat down to eat, Lexie assumed her usual position at the man's feet. She heard them chattering and laughing, and she dozed off and on, waking up every time a morsel of their dinner fell within munching distance. Her family had some friends over and that made for an even better evening. A very enjoyable dinner was followed by watching a beautiful sunset. Afterwards, plates and glasses began making their way into the house, and the bugs started to make an appearance.

This was the time of the day that Lexie liked the least. Her family was going inside, leaving her to fend for herself against the biting gnats and flies. Her skin itched all the time from bites she had incurred. In the oppressive heat it was much worse, so she guessed that was one good thing about her nights in the yard. In addition to all the bugs, the cool night air brought temporary relief from the dry, irritated feeling her coat had during the day. She tried to focus on this and settled in for another nights' sleep.

She had no idea how long she had been asleep when she heard a strange noise. She wasn't even really sure what had woken her up until she heard the noise again. She began barking furiously to warn her family that something wasn't right. One thing that Lexie had learned in her years in the yard was that she needed to be a good guard dog, and she was. But then she heard something else. She heard someone say quietly, "Hey baby!" She tipped her head and gave a couple more warning barks. She saw a light in the house come on, and the man peeked out the window. Lexie barked loudly at him, but instead of helping her investigate, the light shut off and Lexie was on her own. Then she heard it again, a loud, low whisper, "Hey Lexie!"

She walked slowly toward the sound of her name being called because she still didn't like the nighttime nearly as much as she liked the daytime. She heard someone say, "Good girl, Baby! How are you, Sugar?" Then she smelled something absolutely delicious, even better than the little scraps she had gotten from her family that evening. She sniffed the air and got just a little bit closer. Through the pitch blackness she began to make out faces. It looked like a man and a woman, and the woman was holding her hand out. That must have been where the yummy treat was because Lexie could really smell that goodness now! She edged a bit closer, and as she was about to get a taste of whatever was in the woman's hand, she felt something tighten around her neck. She tried to fling her head around to see who was holding her, but all of a sudden she was pulled with such force that it dragged her off her feet.

She had no idea what was happening. She cried and barked and thrashed her body around in an attempt to free herself. The man and woman struggled to control her. Lexie was able to get her feet back on the ground and dig in and she tried to bark, but whatever they had placed around her neck turned her bark into a raspy cry. She pulled back some more and then the man brought his hand closer to her to try and regain control. She panicked and lashed out to bite him wherever she could. Out of the corner of her eye she saw something going toward her belly and felt a sharp pain when the kick was delivered. She cried out and became even more desperate.

The man pulled her relentlessly toward something she couldn't see. The woman was saying something and crying, and Lexie couldn't tell what the man was saying to her but it wasn't nice. Lexie had never been so afraid. Whatever was around her neck was so tight now that Lexie felt like her eyes were going to explode. She couldn't breathe but she struggled on. She wasn't sure how many times she felt a pain in her sides, but she knew that she wanted nothing more than for her family to hear what was going on. She wanted her man to come out and deliver some sharp pain of his own to these people. She wanted him to scare them the way they were scaring her until they took whatever it was off of her neck and ran away—the way she was trying to run away. Then her man would take her into one of those soft, tall beds, and for the first time, she would cuddle and snore and feel safer than she had ever felt in her life.

Instead, the tightness of whatever was around her neck began to get the better of her. She tried to remain aware of what was going on around her. She tried to remain strong and continue her resistance. But in the end she became too dizzy and weak to fight, and she allowed them to pull her to the thing she couldn't see. Even as they were dragging her, she tried to dig her feet into the ground, but eventually they hauled her to an old van. She weakly looked around and saw the man open the back door. She tried to find another surge of strength and whipped her head and neck, trying to loosen their grasp on her. Instead, she got another kick and then the man and woman hoisted her up off of the ground and hurled her through the open door. The most forbidding sound she'd ever heard was the door slamming behind her.

Whatever was around her neck loosened, and she panted and tried to focus on her surroundings. She heard the two get into the van in front of her, and she didn't like the sound of their voices at all. She peed on herself a little bit—she didn't want to, but she couldn't help it. There were all kinds of smells in this van, but these were not comforting smells. She could tell that other dogs had peed on themselves in that van, too. The van started moving, and she heard the familiar crunch of gravel underneath that reminded her so much of home. The pain in Lexie's heart was unimaginable.

She pictured herself back in her pen, complaining to herself about the bug bites and the fact that her bed wasn't as soft or as tall as the ones in the house. She pictured herself only hours before lying at her man's feet and gobbling up treats that had mistakenly—and not mistakenly—been dropped for her. She pictured herself waiting at the edge of the yard for her girls to come home and playing ball in the sun until her back sizzled and her mouth was dry and hot. She listened to the gruff, crude voices and wondered when she would hear the soft-spoken woman again.

Lights started to flicker through the van as they drove past lights on the quiet road. Lexie was terrified and hadn't noticed that she had company. Out of the corner of her eye, she saw a pair of eyes staring at her through the darkness. She watched that spot until another light whisked through the van. Those eyes belonged to a dog that Lexie guessed was about half her age. She sniffed the air at him to try and get a response. The dog was in a cage, and he was pressed as flat to the floor as he could get. His eyes were as large as saucers, staring at her in the dimness. Lexie's heart beat very fast; she continued to pant and realized that her paw pads were sweating. She didn't mean to, but she peed a little more. She should have felt ashamed, but her fear overrode her humiliation. She didn't want to know what was waiting for her and this scared, saucer-eyed dog at the end of the ride.

•••

Lexie would never see her girls or her family again. She would never know how her girls cried for months after she was gone. She would never know how her man wondered what she was trying to tell him with her warning barks, and how he wished he would have gone outside to see for himself what was wrong. She would never know how the girls spent hours and hours hanging signs on posts around the road where they lived, around the roads that intersected that road, and around the towns that these roads led into. On the signs were Lexie's photo, a desperate plea for her return, and a phone number that people called three times with information about a dog that was never Lexie. Dinners outside were never quite the same, and almost a year to the day after Lexie went missing, the family welcomed another four-legged member to the family. Lexie would have been very happy to know that this new pup, Scarlet, got to sleep with her dear girls, safely inside on one of those soft, tall beds.

5

jane

Life had become very business as usual in our home. Foster was still guard dog extraordinaire, I had finished my biology degree and was trying to figure out what I was supposed to do with it, and Brian had left his private investment firm to work at a hedge fund with offices in the Twin Cities and London. It was an incredibly demanding position that required a lot of travel and long hours, but we thought that it was a good rung to climb on the ladder, so he dealt with the stress as well as he could. Tyra was still hanging right in there with us. She was a ripe old eighteen years and still in reasonably good shape for a cat that age. She and Foster maintained their uneasy alliance, and every once in a while we'd walk into the bathroom to see Tyra snuggled up to the heat vent (her most favorite napping spot of all) with Foster lying about six inches behind her. Foster would look up at us, and you could hear him thinking "LOOK HOW CLOSE I AM!!!!" He loved his private time with Tyra, and I'm convinced she just pretended she never had any idea he was there.

When we got Foster, we thought the only two ways that people got dogs and cats were by taking in strays or adopting them from the humane society. We knew we were interested in a Rottweiler, but we didn't see any coming through the shelter. Brian was looking online one day and found a local rescue called "A Rotta Love." They were a group of women committed to Rottweiler and Pit Bull education and rehoming. There was a pit bull named Henna that was absolutely adorable, but in typical Brian-and-Cindy fashion, by the time we were ready to adopt, she had already found a home. There was a scruffy Rottweiler named Jane, though.

I'm not sure what drew us to Jane. Her pictures certainly weren't the cutest, and the bio that had been compiled for her wasn't nearly as witty or compelling as what had been written about most of the other available dogs. It said she was about one year old. She had been found wandering around the Lake Street area of Minneapolis, which is a colorful area of the city that was and is still undergoing a revival of its own. Its history is rich, and the houses were grand at one point, but urban decay had worn the area to a façade of its glory days. Jane had an equal chance of finding someone who wanted to help her, and someone who wanted to harm her. Much to our fortune, she was found by someone who wanted to help.

Jane was found with no collar and no microchip. It was apparent that she had been an outdoor dog because of her thick, coarse coat, and it was likely that her original owner wanted to breed her, but then let her loose when they realized she was the runt. I don't know what it was about Jane, but for whatever reason, one Saturday night after sharing a bottle of wine we submitted our application for her. She was being fostered in a small town north of the Cities, and soon after applying we got an e-mail thanking us for our interest and asking if we would like to set up a meet and greet for us, Foster, and Jane the Rottweiler?

We arrived with Foster in tow to find a ratty, fuzzy little girl waiting for us in her foster family's driveway. Her foster mom had her on a leash attached to her army green and pink "Adopt Me" collar. It's a common collar for foster dogs to wear when waiting for adoption and one that is pretty effective if you ask me. Introductions were made, and Amanda, Jane's foster mom, herded us all into the back yard and showed us Jane's various tricks, including one where Jane remained completely motionless and fixated upon Amanda while she spit hot dogs into Jane's mouth. (To be honest, I still don't understand that one.) Then Amanda led Brian, Foster, Jane, and I on our maiden walk together.

Jane was a professional on that walk. The volunteers and foster families that agree to work with these adoptable dogs spend countless hours in training, both professional and in the home, to make sure these dogs that have so much to lose after placement put their very, very best paw forward. Jane was calm and agile, walking right by our side and taking in the Minnesota landscape that was so different from the streets where she was found. We relished this experience as it was unlike anything we had ever had with Foster.

Would it be surprising to hear that Foster came into his own on that walk, that his maybe-sister calmed him down and he walked patiently by our side, as if taking her cue? Well, in all fairness, for that one walk, that's exactly what happened. Foster appeared to be breathing in the country air, checking in with Brian and I, and interestingly, checking in with this tattered little girl about six feet to his right. He had never been so calm.

Things were shaken up when, at one point during our half-mile or so journey, a large dog came running across a front yard off-leash, head-on toward us, Foster, and Jane. It happened so fast—I'm not sure how long I held my breath. A million scenarios can play out in your mind over the course of a few seconds, but what happened was as non-dramatic as anything you could hope for. Amanda broke from our pack, calmly walked forward, put her arm straight out with her hand in a fist, and said in a low, calm voice, "No!" Just like that the dog retreated. No pomp, no circumstance. And that is when we realized how valuable it was to speak the language of "Dog." Be calm, be cool, be in control, and most importantly, don't ever let them see you holding your breath.

The meet and greet went well. Amanda told us she would be in contact with the rescue director to talk about how things went, and one of them would let us know if we passed the test. If we passed, we would get the final inspection—a home visit. We were nervous but smitten with this little fur ball, so we shook hands, gave kisses to Jane, said our thanks and our good-byes. We were walking down the driveway, and Brian and I turned to sneak in one last peak before we got in the car. Amanda and Jane had stopped and were looking at us from the front porch; Jane wanted one last peak too.

The e-mail came on July 16, 2008. The title was "Hey future family!:)" That was how we found out that Jane was coming home. We still had the home visit to pass, but while our house was on the small side, it was cute and tidy with more than adequate space allotted for Foster, Tyra, and now Jane. We also had a reasonably large fenced yard that we hoped would reflect positively on their opinion. We were hoping that we could get everything out of the way in the morning so that we'd have the rest of the day to get to know Jane and help her get settled. But Amanda and her husband were going to a Neil Diamond concert in St. Paul (jealous) on the Sunday of our scheduled, pending adoption, so in order to avoid having them come to Minneapolis, go back home, then come back to St. Paul that evening, we had to sit and stew and worry about how the visit was going to go until five that evening.

Foster obviously had forgotten the amazing first impression Jane had made on him because when Amanda and her husband walked Jane through our back gate, Foster got pissed. I don't mean a little bit either. I mean Foster got really, really pissed—to the point that Team Foster had to grab his back legs and pull, and Team Jane had to do the same in order to break up the impromptu dog fight that had broken out on our back steps. Dogs are better than people, though, and just like that they got over it. After that initial spat, Foster and Jane never had any significant issues again. Within minutes, Jane was sniffing her new yard, and Foster had adopted Jane's favorite stuffy toy that was supposed to remind her of her foster family. It took him about three-and-a-half minutes to completely destroy it, and neither Amanda nor her husband tried to hide the distaste on their face. Hopefully, the first impression our family had made was good enough to help us survive the second.

Whether it was Foster's time in the shelter, his age, or his general disposition we'll never know, but Jane fell into life in our house and our lives seamlessly. At the time of Jane's adoption, we were a relatively dog-free neighborhood. Foster had been OK—he looked like a German Shepherd, and as far as the neighbors were concerned, we weren't crazy dog people yet. But once we brought Jane home, let's just say the attitudes changed. Thankfully, there were those who greeted her, asked what her name was, responded with a jovial "Just Jane?" and gave her a pat on the head. But then there were a select few who regarded us as criminals every time we walked our disheveled little rottie past their house. In the very short time that we'd had Jane, we'd grown incredibly fond of her and were devoted to her integration not only into our lives, but also the chemistry of the neighborhood.

We have one neighbor in particular named Shirley, who is as sweet as pie, but who was uncertain of Jane and her disposition until one day I was working in the garden. I was trying to weed and cursing to myself for not watering first because I was getting all plant and no root, so those little bastards would be back again in no time. I thought that Foster and Jane were asleep, so when I heard Shirley talking, I assumed she was talking to me. I stood up, and when I did, I saw Shirley leaning over the fence that separates our yards, Foster's head in one hand, and Jane's in the other. Jane was pressed up against the fence, seated in an adorable side-saddle position that could have melted your heart. Shirley was never afraid of her again. Some of our other neighbors have been a little tougher to sell, but after three years, I think the final one has come around. The last time we saw her she didn't refer to Jane as "that Rottweiler." She referred to her as Jane. It seems a simple thing to consider such a monumental success, but to be sure, a success it was.

As Jane settled into our lives, one trait began to emerge that was a little tough for us to come to terms with. Foster had been with us for about four years, and we assumed that, because he was the older, established dog, he would naturally be the alpha. How wrong we were. It was difficult to watch as Jane took his place guard-dogging at the living room window. If Foster was enjoying a drink of water, Jane and her concrete skull were right there to shove him out of the way, whether or not she actually wanted a drink. If Foster had a toy that Jane wanted, well then, Jane just took it. It was tough for us to see Foster take the back seat, and we mentioned our concerns to our vet, along with our apprehensions regarding the possibility that Foster's feelings were being hurt. She looked at us calmly and gave us a response that immediately and permanently alleviated any worries we had. She said, "If he wanted all that stuff bad enough, he'd fight for it." Made perfect sense to me.

Except for that small negative we were seeing in Jane (or what we perceived to be a negative), the rest was all upside. Jane is, quite simply, the sweetest dog on this planet and, if you ask us, one of the cutest. Her abrasive outdoor fur quickly fell out, revealing a silky-soft coat that's quite unusual for the breed. She exudes charisma and has nailed the art of "puppy dog eyes." She also has a strange affinity for head-butting your legs apart and then planting herself directly underneath you, in that lovable side-saddle position, patiently waiting for a head scratch. Unfortunately, she doesn't care what you're wearing or how tall you are, so this action is either completely endearing or completely awkward. Consider yourself warned if you're under five feet five and/or in a maxi-dress.

2008 came and went, and 2009 was about to bring changes to our family, both good and bad. I had gone back to school (again) in 2005 to get my nursing degree, which I finished in 2007. My dreams of veterinary medicine had been dashed, when, despite the multiple resumes I had sent to various vet clinics, local shelters, etc., the only nibble I got was from one of Brian's clients. She e-mailed him information about a position she had within her company. The position was for a surgical technician in the company's animal testing facility. I know someone's got to do it, but that someone could never be me. Clearly the universe was trying to tell me I was on the wrong path.

So I became an RN (which was a long, arduous, miserable experience that I would never—I repeat NEVER—do again) and got my first nursing job working on the transplant floor at the University of

Minnesota. I cannot finish this without giving a little shout-out to the foot soldiers who are floor nurses. I have never been so stressed; physically, emotionally, and mentally challenged; exhausted; and insecure as I was the first year as a transplant nurse. For all of you nurses who are on the front lines every morning, evening, and night, you have my utmost and total respect. It's a job that until you do it, you'll never understand the incredible responsibility, psychological toll, and difficult decisions you're faced with each and every shift.

Thankfully, Brian had tired of the stress and strain of his position, something that I had waited for since the day he started. Life at a hedge fund is great for some people, but one thing I love about Brian is that as much as he's committed to whatever position he's in, he likes to be able to leave work at work as much as possible. The London office of his firm opened seven hours before the office in the Twin Cities, so every morning Brian's Blackberry began going off at 1 a.m., leaving him e-mails and trades in the double digits that he was technically supposed to handle before he was even awake. Taking time off was next to impossible, and he was going in earlier and earlier and getting home later and later. Enough was enough. He met with the advisor at the private investment firm where he had previously worked. This advisor didn't have anything, but he did know of a different office that may have something. Well that office in Bloomington, a southern suburb of Minneapolis, proved to be a match made in heaven for Brian and, God willing, the place where I hope he'll grow old and retire from.

Being the classic underachiever that I am, I grew tired of the pressures of transplant and found an ad for an ophthalmology outpatient surgery center that needed an RN. I submitted my resume, and the next day I got a phone call to set up a phone interview. The place had a 6 a.m. start (boo) but no holidays, weekends, overnights, poop, puke, code blues...you get where I'm going. So fortunately, by 2009 Brian and I had settled into relatively low-key, stable positions that were much better fits for us both.

Jane continued to be a neighborhood favorite of those who didn't buy into the stereotype of her breed. She even got along relatively well with Tyra. Sweet old Tyra never took a liking to Foster, but for some reason Jane was a little easier to sell. Don't get me wrong, Jane and Tyra were never going to sit down over a cup of coffee, but if Jane had been lying on the bed for more than a half hour and Tyra was fairly certain she wasn't moving, she'd jump up there with her and assume the spot farthest away from Jane. We never got a "Look how close I am!!" look from Jane, probably because she really didn't care how close she was.

One day I went over to pick up Tyra, which she absolutely hated, but because we put the food in her belly, I allowed myself the pleasure once every great while. When I did, I was stunned at how round and taut her belly was. I should have known something was wrong then, and in hindsight I probably did. But she had been eating a lot lately, which wasn't completely unusual for her, so I told myself that she was older and her metabolism was undoubtedly at a standstill, which would explain the huge gut. Had I been thinking rationally, I would have realized that she would have been gaining weight all over and not just in her rock-hard, round tummy. Over the course of the next few weeks, as her abdomen became fuller and rounder, I finally had to admit to myself that something was wrong.

Our trip to the vet confirmed the worst. Tyra had cancer in her spleen, and it would metastasize quickly to other parts of her body. We could try and take the spleen out, but the risks of a surgery that extensive on a cat Tyra's age were great, and the outcomes were likely not to be favorable. The fullness in her belly was due to a buildup of a fluid called ascites. It was likely very uncomfortable for Tyra, but to remove it would be removing proteins from her body which would shorten her time with us. In the end, though, we made the weekly trip to her vet to have her tummy tapped to remove as much of the fluid as was practical. Yes, we wanted her as long as we could have her, but we couldn't stand the thought of how unbearable that bloating must have been.

Tyra declined gradually at first. We could see she was weakening, her appetite was getting worse, and her jet-black coat was again taking on the dusting of flakes that we had seen after we lost Sadie. We had started using puppy pads next to her litter box about six months prior because rather than going in her box, she had taken to going just outside of it. As time went on, the puppy pad use spread nearly all over the house—her incontinence was pronounced. It was becoming evident that a decision needed to be made, and even when the right decision is slapping you in the face, they are still words you never want to speak.

I sat in a chair in the living room one evening; it was one that I favored because it gave me a perfect view of the rug in the kitchen where Tyra liked to sleep. I was crying then, as I'm crying now, and said to Brian, "It should probably be this week." We sat in complete silence, tears running down both of our faces. I would have never believed what happened next if I hadn't experienced it myself.

Brian and I continued to sit, not knowing what to say next. All of a sudden, out of the corner of my eye, I saw Tyra stand up. She made her way over to me, and for the first time in probably ten years, she jumped up into my lap. Brian watched from across the room, his eyes huge. Not only was she not a snuggler, but I have no idea how she found the strength to jump that high; she was having so much difficulty getting around. I sat in stunned silence while she looked me in the eyes. She probably only stayed about two minutes, but I will never forget that moment—how it made me feel, and how much I loved and respected Tyra for telling us that it was OK. We made the heartbreaking appointment for that Thursday.

I was planning on working Monday and Tuesday so that I could spend all day Wednesday loving my girl. When I got home from work that Tuesday, however, I was stunned. I found her in Jane's kennel, which I'd never seen before. She could barely move, and her eyes were unfocused. I felt complete desperation. I don't even know what other word to use. I was furious with myself for not being there when Tyra had been so rapidly deteriorating. I tried to pick her up, and she couldn't hold her neck steady. How long had she been like this, while I was at work, selfishly trying to focus on something that would keep my mind off of our sweet girl? I don't remember calling Brian, but I know that he called me and said he had made the appointment and he was on his way to pick us up. I never got my day with Tyra.

She was with me in four cities, two countries, countless apartments, and finally a home. She was with me during the happy times, the not-so-happy times, and the downright miserable times. She was with me while I kissed a lot of toads until I found my prince. And my prince and I had to say good-bye to our sweet Tyra on February 17, 2009. She was a blessing in my life for nineteen years, and what I wouldn't give for another nineteen.

To Tyra, our little curmudgeon, we miss you so much and hope that we appreciated you enough when we had you. You and your sister changed who I was and who I am as a person. You showed me the strength of the human/animal bond. You showed me that it's OK to love with all of your heart, even if the one you love can't say those words back to you. And you showed me that oftentimes it's even better to see the love in someone's eyes than to hear it from their lips. Because then you know it's true. I love you sweet girl. Sorry about the dogs.

Mourning Tyra was a little different than it had been for Sadie. I felt a finality that I didn't remember feeling with Sadie. Perhaps it was because the last of my girls was gone. It was painful to think back to those days of cuddling on the couch, eating take-out Thai food from the restaurant across the street, watching The X-Files and VHS movies, and knowing they were truly gone forever. I wouldn't have traded my family for anything, but one old saying rang loud, clear, and true: "The only fault of a cat or a dog is they don't live forever."

So, our family had no choice but to soldier on and come to terms with our catless home. Brian had become incredibly allergic to cats in the confined quarters of our Prague flat, and, while being in a larger space had lessened his allergic reactions, he still struggled despite taking medications. So with Tyra's passing came the end of an era in our house. From that point on, we were forced to be crazy dog people.

It was a year or so after we lost our mini-panther that the "biological clock" started ticking again. We discovered that the city of Minneapolis says that you are allowed three animals over the age of four months, and we had only two. We were short a dog. We had our Foster and Jane, and we figured that a pit bull was the next likely step. We checked all the local rescues and found many dogs that were so adorable and likely contenders—that is until the day I went online and read a story that nearly stopped my heart. It was a story that didn't just keep me awake at night, the horror of it woke me up at night.

6

lexie

All the dogs were kept separate from each other. They were in sight, but there was no room for interaction. Her cage was rusty and smelly and her yard was again filled with rocks and dirt, but this time the smells were not interesting or comforting. She had stopped thinking about her mama and siblings long ago. Her stomach was empty almost all the time, and she had quit trying to remember what it was like to have a full belly, too. She had stopped wondering why this had happened.

After that tortuous van ride ended, she never saw the saucer-eyed dog again. The doors had opened onto a scene that reminded her of where she had lived with her beloved family, except for the fact that it filled her completely with fear. As with the smells in the van, she couldn't identify the smells in this place either, but they chilled her to her bones. She whimpered a little that night, but not loudly enough for those people in the front seat to hear. The cage with the saucer-eyed dog had been pulled out of the van, and it crashed to the ground with a loud thud. Some man had been there to drag the crate across the yard, pulling up some of what little grass there was. The saucer-eyed dog didn't face Lexie as he was pulled away, but she knew his expression had remained exactly the same. Lexie's turn was next, and the woman put that tightness around her neck and dragged her out of the van too.

Lexie didn't know what to hope for—or if she could hope for anything at all. She realized that the more she resisted, the tighter that thing got around her neck. It seemed fruitless to fight, so Lexie hesitantly walked behind the woman, fearful, sniffing what she could, but processing nothing. It seemed like they walked for a long time before she began hearing barks and cries. She didn't have much experience with other dogs, other than the occasional rogue who made its way into her yard. She wasn't sure how much she liked the sounds that she was hearing.

As they got closer, she made out a large building that didn't look like the house where her cherished family lived, nor did it look like the house where she had lived underneath the porch with her mama. This place looked big and plain. It had one small door on the side they were approaching. She could really hear those dogs now, and she didn't like it one bit. She knew she should be scared, but she was so intimidated and overwhelmed that she didn't feel much of anything. She knew she was hungry, and she knew she needed to relieve herself, but she was too frightened of this woman to think it was OK to do this in front of her. She sniffed around as they approached the building and saw lots of chains in the yard. She had only been tied to a chain once after she had wandered off, and she didn't like how heavy and restrictive it had felt. She saw lots of tires and other things she had never seen before.

They reached the door to the large, plain building, and the barking sounded almost like screams. She had never heard sounds like that in her life. Lexie still felt overwhelmed, but now she could feel the fear building with every beat of her heart. The woman opened the door, and the smells of urine, feces, and something else she didn't recognize overcame Lexie. The sounds were loud and frantic and Lexie had never, ever felt terror like she felt now, even when that man and woman had dragged her to the van. She began resisting again, so the woman pulled her through the door into the dimly lit space.

The room was huge and tall, and she could see cages stacked everywhere. They were along the walls, down the center, in corners, stacked one on top of the other. As the woman pulled her across the floor, Lexie vaguely remembered looking into those cages. Some of the eyes looking back at her were hungry and frightened. Some of the eyes were angry. All of them looked lost. Lexie's tethered journey ended at a cage somewhere near the farthest corner of the room. There was only one light that was intended to light the whole area, and it was a good distance away from her, so it was difficult to see. The woman opened the cage and thrust Lexie inside. She offered little resistance. To be honest, being in that cage seemed safer than being with that woman, out amongst the crates filled with desperate dogs.

Her leg had brushed against a bowl when she was pushed inside, but when she investigated, it was empty. She didn't feel like eating anyway. She circled in this cage and wondered if her family had noticed she was missing yet. The pang in her heart at the thought of them was indescribable. Her fear and apprehension mixed with an emotion that she had never felt so strongly, even when she was taken from her mama— she felt homesick. She would give anything to be home in her soft bed with the flies and gnats giving her a nighttime reprieve. Instead, she herself now had saucer-eyes as she tried to look around the faintly lit room. "This," she thought to herself, "is as bad as it gets."

Lexie was able to doze for a couple of minutes at a time, but she always awoke with a start, her anxiety and horror returning when she realized she didn't know where she was, why she was there, or what was going to happen to her. She still hadn't relieved herself and hoped that someone would be around to help her soon. She didn't like these people that brought her here, but she really needed to go, and her cage was simply not big enough for her to turn the other cheek and make her bladder and bowels happy. She whined a little bit, but nothing that compared with the racket the other dogs were making. She tried to close her eyes and forget about how uncomfortable she was, realizing quickly that wouldn't be possible. She stood up and began pacing in circles in her small area. She really, really needed to go, so she began barking. Her barks mixed with all the others to form a tragic, off-key symphony that would go unnoticed unless their captors needed them for something—and Lexie still didn't know what that something was.

The man thought about the two dogs they had gotten that night. The younger one he was sure would be a clown dog—a dog used for the fighting dogs to practice on—and they were a dime a dozen. They cost next to nothing to feed, so it was always good to have a few on hand. Keeping the clown weak and hungry made it that much easier to get a good battle out of the fighter. If the clown dog got sick or a wound got infected, well then, all the better. The fighters were on that shit like white on rice.

He wasn't sure about the bitch, though. She was a decent size, probably about fifty to sixty sturdy pounds. She was the older of the two, and if she wasn't a good fighter, then maybe she'd produce some good fighting puppies. At the very least he'd have another clown.

He looked over at his wife who was sleeping. He was sorry he'd gotten cross with her because he appreciated her going with him on trolls. Most wives and girlfriends were tolerant of the dogs, but he didn't know any that were willing to participate in the catch. But like it or not, he believed a man and a woman driving around at 3 a.m. with a van full of dogs didn't look as suspicious as a man driving alone. She just got so damned excited about nothing, and that shit was going to drum up some trouble if she didn't learn to quiet down. The dogs were going to fight back some; they wouldn't want them if they didn't. She'd never been bitten, and he'd told her time and time again that he'd kill any fucker that did bite her. He sighed. He would have given her a kiss, but he didn't want to wake her up, so he rolled over and went to sleep.

Lexie was mortified. She had pleaded and pleaded for someone to come and let her out until finally she couldn't hold it any longer. She went as far into the corner of her tiny cage as she could and allowed her bladder and bowels to empty. That horrific act, coupled with the dim light and constant din of barks, screams, and cries, had put her in a mild state of shock. She retreated to the opposite corner to avoid the mess she'd made, but it was spreading across the floor, and she could feel it under her legs and the pads of her feet. She didn't know what to do, so she closed her eyes and pretended that she could feel her soft bed under her instead of her own waste. "This," she thought to herself, "is as bad as it gets."

7

the wooded area

Lexie was exhausted when two men pulled her from the kennel that morning. One was the man who had shoved her into the van the night before, and the other—well, she didn't like the looks of him any better than she had liked the first. They took her outside, past where she had seen the tires. There were more trees here, and she was grateful for the shade because the early morning sun had felt like fire on her eyes, emerging from the faint light of her overnight prison. She wished she would have been able to hold out long enough to relieve herself here.

She heard barking as they approached a wooded area, but the barking all but stopped when Lexie and the men became visible. There were probably seven or eight other dogs there, and they had the same scared, hungry, lost look as the other dogs she had seen. The men put one of those heavy chains around her neck, and she felt as though she would never be able to breathe again. She looked up at the men, imploring them to give her a reason why she was there. Her tail was glued between her legs, and her eyes revealed her distress. Her stomach was growling so loudly, but there was no food anywhere to put in it.

The other dogs were quieter there than they were in the room. The air was fresher too, so if she had to pick a place, she supposed this was much better than staying in that small cage that was covered in her waste. It was somewhat comforting to know that if she needed to relieve herself, there was a patch of grass nearby for her to use. The chain around her neck was so heavy and so tight, though, that walking even a short distance was arduous. She looked around at the other dogs, and they looked at her. She felt scared, but here in the fresh air her exhaustion got the better of her, and she closed her eyes.

She woke to a bowl being thrown in front of her. She looked around, and most of the other dogs had bowls too. Those that didn't looked on with heavy eyes and sorrow while hungry mouths devoured whatever those bowls contained. Some of the unlucky ones gave a half-hearted tail wag and looked at the men, thinking they deserved a meal too. They didn't. Lexie looked down, and her bowl contained some water, but not much. There was dirt at the bottom of the bowl, and a few scattered leaves, but she was thirsty so she drank all she could. The same two men stood near her and appeared to be sizing her up. She whined just a little to let them know how disappointed she was that she hadn't gotten any food. One of the men barked something at her, and the same man that had forced her into the van last night gave her side another good kick. She yelped from the shock of it, and he kicked her again. That time, she was silent.

Lexie grew weaker and weaker. She spent most of her time on that chain, which, with next-to-no food in her belly, became even more difficult to handle. On any given day or night, dogs were taken off their chains to go who knew where. Sometimes they came back; often they were never seen again. The dogs that did come back scared Lexie nearly to death. Some were able to walk; many were not. So the men would carry them, drop them to the ground, and put those heavy chains back around their necks. Lexie would watch as the men walked away.

The dogs either breathed very hard or almost not at all. They were bloody, and it was in the wooded area where she recognized that third smell that she hadn't been able to identify on the first night when she was hauled into that room. It was blood. The dogs' ears were ripped open, or their teeth had gone through their lips. Sometimes when they returned, their faces were unrecognizable. Those days that the dogs came back, Lexie would flatten herself to the ground and try not to think about how much she missed her sweet girls, her man, and the soft-spoken woman.

One evening she was on her chain. She had been looking for squirrels (which seemed to have retired for the night) and chewing on some rocks that had become her version of a chew toy. She hadn't eaten in a long time. Unexpectedly, she saw three men walk into the wooded area. Her ears dropped and her tail tucked when she didn't see them carrying a food bucket. If men came into the area where the dogs were on chains and didn't have any food for them, well, then someone was going to be taken off of the chain and taken away. She tried to become invisible.

She recognized two of the men, but one of them was a stranger. They walked over to her and removed her chain. The terror began in her heart and spread immediately all through her body. She began shaking, and her legs became cold and numb. She completely flattened herself against the ground as though her legs had simply stopped working. The men put a tether around her neck similar to the one they had used to drag her into the van weeks ago. They pulled her along the ground, and she could feel the rocks scraping underneath her belly, though she paid no attention to whether the rocks hurt her or not. Her mind reeled, dreading what might come next.

They hadn't given her much thought. Bitches not born into this typically didn't have a lot of fight in them, but she had a good size and body, so why not see what she had? They had a dog that showed some promise, so this was a win/win for them. Either they got to see how much spunk this bitch had, or the other dog would get a good workout, and they'd see what he was really made of.

They dragged her to a different area close to where she was kept on the chain, but far enough away that it felt very different. She smelled the third smell—blood—really clearly. Lots of people filled the room, and she could hear chatter and laughter. One of the men moved in to try and pick her up, and his sudden movement caused her to lash out. He was startled and struck her across her snout, and her fear and instinct caused her to bare her teeth and try to defend herself again. This time the blow he delivered hurt her, a lot. She felt his fury as he picked her up as though she weighed nothing at all and threw her over a short wall.

She was dazed when she landed on her side in a small pen. She tried to make out her surroundings, but between the terror in her heart and the pain in her head it was nearly impossible for her to focus. She heard another dog, and it sounded like it was in the same pen with her. She looked up over the bones that protruded where her belly used to be and saw the dog opposite of her in the pen. She could see it was on a leash and that the leash was strained. The dog didn't look angry to her, only curious and confused. She tried to clear her head and made her way to her feet. There was a man she'd never seen before holding the leash of the other dog, and as she stood, she saw him drop the leash.

The dog careened across the pen toward her, and instinct replaced her fear. Her ears went back and she bared her teeth. The other dog appeared somewhat surprised and changed his position as well. His head hung lower and his pace slowed. He bared his teeth and growled so low in his throat that she could feel every beat of her heart. She could hear the men around the pen cheering, and this appeared to boost the dog's confidence because all of a sudden he had two legs over top of her and her thick neck roll in his mouth, tearing at her flesh. She cried out and tried to turn her head to protect herself, but his jaw was strong. The cheering intensified. The dog had managed to push her to her side, ripping at her ears and snout. She could never have imagined that much pain in the whole world. The cheers of the crowd and the vicious growls of her attacker drowned out her cries. She tasted blood in her throat, and then she saw nothing.

8

the skinny brown dog

It was impossible to remember that another life had ever existed. Her family that she never, ever thought about anymore wouldn't have recognized her as their Lexie. Her legs bore large and permanent scars from the urine and feces that sat at the bottom of her cage, breaking her skin down over the years. There wasn't one part of her face that didn't have an old wound on it, and her belly hung low from the many pregnancies she'd had. Unlike the three precious litters she had given birth to with her family, these litters caused her nothing but indescribable heartbreak.

Her puppies were always taken from her far too soon, and she didn't know which was worse, knowing they were tossed into the pit for practice—as she had been more times than she ever wanted to remember—or meeting them years down the road, after they'd been trained by these monsters to inflict as much damage to her as they could. She had no doubt they recognized her, but they had no choice; it was what the monsters forced them to do. The attacks were no easier to endure when they came from her own blood; in fact, they were much more difficult. She liked to imagine her litters that she'd had so long ago. Those puppies were grown now and living in a yard of their own, taking rides in big green trucks and maybe, just maybe, sleeping right this second on one of those tall, soft beds. With these babies, though, she was forced to see the truth. Because of her, they were forced to endure a life of hell.

She should have fought harder on that day that she refused to remember. She should never have allowed herself to be dragged into that van. If she hadn't, then these babies would be safe with a family that loved them the way she had once been loved. Instead, on more than one occasion, one of them stood across the pen from its mother, whose legs had been bound to ensure that she couldn't fight back, and waited for the order to attack. The shame of it all almost took her breath away, and she tried to will to them that she still loved them, and that she was so, so sorry.

She wasn't sure how many litters of pups she'd had, but as long as she lived, she'd never forget the disgrace and agony of how the monsters forced her babies into the world. Every time she saw that sling, her body went limp. When it was time to put babies in her belly again—and it seemed like it was always that time—the men took her and put her head and legs in the trusses on a stand near the pit that caused her so much agony. Once she was secured to the sling, dog after dog came and mounted her so that she could continue to produce precious pups that these monsters would brutalize in the most inhumane ways. It was always painful, and in the beginning she had tried to fight back. She always wanted to fight back and demand the dignity and love she once had, but the monsters didn't allow it. On the sole occasion where she had had enough and tried to attack one of her "suitors," her world changed in a way that could never be changed back.

She was enduring the pain and shame of the rape when all of a sudden the memories of her previous life pounded into her conscience. She remembered the earthy, musty smell of her home underneath the porch that she shared with her mama and siblings. She remembered that first ride home with her new family and how much she liked the music they had been playing and the way they looked at her with kind eyes. She remembered sleeping on her bed in her yard full of dirt and rocks that was so much different than the hellish plot of dirt and rocks she was looking at now. She remembered feeling angry about the bugs and stealing scraps of food that had fallen to her man's feet at meal-time. And then she remembered her girls. She remembered them lying on her stomach, telling her their secrets in the sunshine. She remembered them burying their faces in her thick neck roll which soaked up all their tears—the same neck roll that now had fresh cuts on top of old scars. She remembered playing in the yard with them, running in the sun until her back sizzled and her mouth felt hot and dry. And even though she knew she would never go back to them, she felt that she had to fight for them one last time.

The rage that welled up from the bottom of her throat surprised even her. She howled ferociously and tried with all of her strength to throw the dog off of her. She bared her teeth and her mouth started to foam. She knew it was the time to rise up and try to make right some of the unforgiveable wrongs that she had suffered. She tried to twist her body but quickly realized that whatever the slings were secured to was too heavy for her to move. She tried twisting the other way and then tried simply throwing herself over in hopes that she might be able to get some ground under her feet, but she was helpless. Knowing how truly vulnerable she was, she launched into a frenetic episode trying to defend herself from the now-furious dog that had been brought in to mount her. The dog had begun attacking her in a flurry of teeth and fur when all of a sudden one of the men pulled him off of her. She had felt blows and kicks from these men before. But nothing, absolutely nothing compared to the kick that she got squarely on the left side of her head directly over her ear. She heard a loud ringing and then her body slumped, seemingly lifeless in the slings.

She was out, but they gave her one more kick for good measure. It wasn't often that a bitch had a bit of fight in her after this long. She was strong, though, and they couldn't afford her doing any damage to a potential prize dog. They brought her to the ground, and one of the men held her mouth open. The other got a pair of rusty pliers and began pulling her teeth, one by one. The small teeth up front were never a big deal. They came out with a little twist and pull—sometimes two came out at once if things went well. The canines, though, were always tougher. The men twisted and pulled, but all they could manage was to break one of them, and it wasn't even a good break. Blood hung from her mouth in crimson strings. They grabbed a file, similar to those used on horses' hooves, and started roughly filing the canines that they couldn't pull. She started to stir by the time they finished, so they dragged her back to her cage and threw her inside.

•••

She had no idea how many days and nights had passed. She hadn't been thrown into the pit for awhile and while she was grateful for that, the pain she felt in her mouth was constant. She was back in her cage and her fitful dreams were interrupted early one evening when she woke to one of the men staring at her through the bars of her cage. Even with as much pain as she had experienced in her life in hell, she never imagined that she could feel like this. If she could have willed herself to stop breathing, she would have. She peered up with huge, fearful eyes, hoping the monster had brought her something to eat. Her mouth hurt tremendously, but her tummy growled, and sometimes, if she had a little food to put in her belly, it helped her sleep, just for a little while—though sleep had quit providing her sweet dreams about her family a lifetime ago. The worst dreams of all were when she could feel herself at her man's feet, listening to the clinking of ice in glasses, the laughter of her family, and the wind in her overturned ear. Then the dream would inevitably turn to dogs entering the yard, attacking her. Her soul would come crashing down when she woke and saw that she was still in the hellish abyss.

Looking up at the man, she could tell he hadn't brought her something to put in her empty stomach, and she knew immediately that something was different. She had been experiencing horrors at this man's hands for as long as she could remember, and her most valuable skill was her ability to retreat deep inside herself when something bad was about to happen. And, for what could have been the millionth time, she knew something very bad was about to happen.

The man flung open her cage and grabbed her by the rope that he used as her collar. She couldn't help herself and peed just a little bit. He pulled her to the floor and began to examine her closely. He pried open her mouth and appeared satisfied. Her mouth hurt her so, and she didn't understand why that made him happy, but then the skinny dog would never understand why the man did the things he did. When the man grabbed pieces of rope very similar to the rope around her neck, the skinny dog went numb. He tied her front legs together, and he tied her back legs together, and the skinny dog didn't cry or plead. Her eyes simply went blank. She didn't care what happened to her.

Old wounds reopened and her legs started bleeding–they hadn't healed from the last time she was bound up and thrown in the pit. Then, something happened that even she had never experienced. The skinny dog was lying helpless and hopeless, her eyes fixed in a blank stare that would have shattered the heart of anyone who had a heart. She was desperately trying to hide deep inside herself when she felt a sharp pain in her leg that she had never felt before. The skinny dog was always so quiet, but the shock of the cut was enough to make her scream in pain. She felt a blow to her face, and then she went quiet again. She could hear the dogs in the pit barking and crying, and she could hear people laughing and cheering. She had heard all of this before, but she could tell that something was different.

Her mouth was sore and her leg was cut. She was dazed and terrified. The man grabbed her by her front and hind legs and threw her scarred and battered body into the bloodied pit. She urinated uncontrollably and heard the people laughing at her. She heard the dog across the pit and tried to pretend that she was somewhere else. She pretended that she was back in her cage and that the man had instead brought her a small meal. She pretended that her mouth didn't hurt and that her leg wasn't cut. She pretended that the dog that was about to attack her was safely back in his cage with a small meal, too. He didn't want to be doing this to the skinny dog—she knew it. He was simply doing what the man had told him he had to do. She didn't even know the dog had been released until she felt the horrors of the attack begin, and she knew what was different. She knew that finally, mercifully, this life was over.

9

no dog left behind

It was a heady evening for the man. His dog had done good. He hadn't done perfect, but he'd done good. Some of the folks stopped by to congratulate him on the promise his fighter showed. Others who had been dogmen lots longer stopped to offer tips. He felt giddy with the potential of this dog, and if it continued, all the prime babies he'd be able to get from him. He went over to his fighter and rewarded him with some kibble and a scratch on the head. The fighter still had blood on his face and legs, but the vast majority of it wasn't his blood. He wagged his tail and looked up at the man with hopeful eyes. The dog loved it when he had done something to make the man happy.

The clown lay almost motionless in the pit, save her belly which was slightly swollen with the babies it contained. If he would have had more luck with the babies this clown had produced in the past, he never would have thrown her in the pit tonight. But she was old, and he was sure she didn't have much, if any, potential left. Plus, the fact that she was old just built his fighter's confidence. The belly with the babies shallowly rose and fell with her breaths. His cousin had always told him, if they were going to pass, get rid of them. No dog left behind. Should the cops ever show up, there's no way to pass off a dead dog; it's hard enough to explain away an injured one. And don't bother burying them. Either one of the other dogs would find them, or the cops would notice the freshly turned dirt. Some of the cops don't mind a little dog rolling, but some of them don't like it, and it wasn't worth the risk.

The man threw some tarp down in the back of his van. It was the same van that the clown had been forced into four years ago—four years ago when her name was Lexie. When she was Lexie, this dog had known love. She had felt safe in her backyard with her family and her girls. She had chased balls in the sun until her back sizzled and her mouth felt hot and dry. She had lain at her man's feet listening to the happy chatter of her family and waited for a wayward morsel that she could devour before anyone noticed. The dog named Lexie had never known that evil existed in her world.

The man walked over and picked up the skinny brown dog. He'd had this clown longer than he'd had any other. She was a tough bitch, but she never showed enough gameness to be of much use to him. He'd gotten some decent pups from her, though, so he supposed he appreciated that. He picked up her almost lifeless body. She probably wouldn't make it much longer than a couple of hours; his fighter had done a number on her. He didn't bother untying her legs. He had put coveralls over his clothes before he picked her up, but he was probably going to have to throw them away when he was finished. She was a fucking mess. The blood was bad enough, but it wasn't worth trying to wash the piss and shit out of them. They were an old pair anyway. He walked over to the van, tossed her on the tarp, and slammed the door. What once had been the most forbidding sound she'd ever heard went almost unnoticed. The skinny dog once known as Lexie slipped in and out of consciousness.

She had been brought into this world knowing the love of a mother and seven siblings, born sixth in her litter during that singular hour where anything is possible and everything is imaginable. Her thick brown neck roll had soaked up the tears of her girls, and her now torn and bloody ears had listened to their secrets. This dog, like every dog, was born to love and be loved.

The man threw her to the side of the road, left to die alone and in pain. And she didn't care. She heard the crickets and felt a pain in her heart. Then there was pain with every breath in and every breath out. The pain was physical, and it was something else. The pain wasn't for one thing in particular. It was for all the pain she had ever suffered, and it was the worst pain she had ever felt. And then, she felt nothing.

10

i'll be there soon

Son of a bitch. She'd been late two other days this week and now she couldn't find her keys. Diane had made it more than clear that she wasn't putting up with this much longer. She needed this job, too. The hours weren't great and she really didn't love retail, but her Mom always said if you have a reason to set your alarm clock and get up in the morning, consider yourself lucky. Where the hell had she put them? She frantically retraced her steps and somehow found them in the linen closet. She must have set them in there when she grabbed some Kleenex for her purse.

She checked the front door to make sure it was locked and started out. The sun was already high in the sky for seven o'clock; she could tell it was going to be a beautiful day. She turned on the car and "Airplanes" by B.o.B was on the radio. "Fucking LOVE this song," she thought to herself. It was going to be a good day. She was driving along, watching the sunlight cut through the trees, singing along with Hayley Williams's part of the song, and thinking she sounded pretty damn good, thank you very much. She was tapping her hands on the steering wheel when she noticed something alongside the road.

"Sweet Jesus, that's the biggest raccoon I've ever seen," she thought. She slowed, and as she was just about to pass the animal, she looked in horror as she realized it was a dog. She slowed the car until it eventually stopped twenty-five feet directly across from the dog. She looked in her rearview mirror. No one was behind her, so she looked again at the dog with a mixture of horror and indecision. What the hell had happened to it? It probably was hit by a car, but Jesus, that car must have been going ninety. What if the dog was dead? She couldn't just leave it there. Holy shit, what if the dog was alive? What the hell was she supposed to do with it? Her mind was racing and her palms were a little sweaty. She couldn't sit in the middle of the road, so she backed up and pulled in just behind the dog. She knew she'd be in trouble, but she got out her cell phone and dialed work.

"Lisa, it's Missy. Listen, I'm on 102 right outside of Westerfield, and there's a dog on the side of the road."

"And?"

"And" was right. At the risk of sounding repetitive, what the hell was she supposed to do?

"I know Diane's going to be pissed, but I can't just leave this animal here. I'm going to see if it's still alive and figure out what to do from there, but I'll probably be a little late. Just tell her I'm sorry, and I'll get there as soon as I can."

"You got that right. Diane will be pissed. I'll tell her, but you're on your own with this one." Missy rolled her eyes. Lisa was usually abrupt, but for once in her life she could quit being a bitch and offer some support, or at the very least not make Missy feel guilty for wanting to do the right thing.

"I'll get there as soon as I can. I promise. Thanks, Lisa."

"Don't thank me. I didn't do anything. And being a Good Samaritan's only going to get you so far. You remember that. I'd get here soon if I were you."

"I'll be there soon. Thanks."

The entire time Missy had been on the phone, her gaze had been fixed on the dog. She had been raised with dogs her whole life and had a huge soft spot for them in her heart. She began to slowly get out of the car. Her legs were shaking as she stood and took a deep breath before making her way to the animal. Her breathing got heavier, and her heart began pounding. She didn't know which would be better—if the dog was dead or alive. If the dog was dead, she could at least go get a shovel and blanket and bury it to the side of the road where it wouldn't get hit again. Ashes to ashes she believed. But, what if it was alive? As she approached the dog, what she saw surprised her so much that when she inhaled, her breath stuck in her throat as though she would suffocate. She tried to exhale and couldn't. She realized with absolute revulsion that this dog had not been hit by a car. She knew this because as she drew closer, she saw that the dog's legs weren't simply stretched out. She could see that its legs had been tied.

She reached the dog and knelt down. Seeing the dog close up was shocking, and she knew that the image of this dog lying bloody, bound, and discarded on the side of 102 would be forever seared into her memory. She leaned close to the dog and watched and listened for signs of life. Sure enough, a tiny blood bubble inflated and deflated on its nose with each labored and superficial breath she took. Missy could tell the dog was a female because the dog's belly appeared to have a litter in it. Dear God, this dog was alive.

She kneeled closer and stared at the dog's wounded face and scarred, ripped-up body. Tears burned her eyes and blurred her vision, and the feeling of suffocation returned, not because she couldn't breathe, but because a lump had grown in her throat that was so large it actually hurt. She wiped her eyes and her nose on her shirt and thought for a minute how pissed Diane was going to be when she blew in to work looking like she'd been on a bender. She felt like laughing deliriously until the gravity of the situation hit her again, hard.

What the hell—or maybe more importantly, who the hell—had happened to this dog? She reached out and gently touched the dog's head. She probably should have been afraid the dog was aggressive, but one, she looked to be on the verge of death, and two, Missy couldn't help but reach out to this poor soul who was obviously suffering. Her gasp could have been heard up and down that quiet highway when the dog responded to her soft touch by raising her head just a little, opening her eyes, and giving Missy a vacant look.

Missy panicked. Tears streaked her face as she ran back to the car to retrieve her cell. She caught a glimpse of herself in the rearview mirror as she reached for the phone on the dash. Her face was blotchy and red and stained with mascara, and her eyes were so bloodshot she didn't think a bottle of Visine for each of them would do any good. "Jesus, I do look like I've been on a bender," she muttered to herself. She began clumsily dialing while she ran back to the dog. She listened to it ring and prayed and prayed she'd get a voice on the other end. There was only one person she felt she could call, and she didn't know what she would do if the only thing she heard on the other end was a voice message.

"Come on, come on, come on..." Missy paced back and forth as she nervously listened to the rings, wiping her nose on her sleeve and staring at the poor dog that was at some point supposed to be a mother.

"Hello?"

"Oh my God, Dad!"

"Missy, what's wrong?" She was crying and he could hear the fear in her voice, which caused his voice to be riddled with it as well. Anytime his daughter called him crying, he assumed she'd either gone into a ditch or had been attacked. He could feel his blood pressure rising immediately.

"I'm on 102 about a mile outside of town—"

"Are you OK? I'm on my way. Just tell me where you are!"

"I told you, on 102. Dad, there's a dog here."

He grabbed a blanket and a knife like she'd asked and made his way the two and a half miles or so to where Missy said she was. She told him the dog was a mess and that her legs were tied up. "Dogfighters," he'd thought to himself. "Doughnuts to fucking dollars that dog was with fighters." Considering the way Missy described the dog's condition, what the hell else could it be? Having been born and raised in the region, he knew how commonplace it was to fight dogs, but he'd never condoned it, nor did he want his family exposed to that kind of degeneracy. They got exposed to enough evil just turning on the God-damned TV. They didn't need to see the remnants of it lying on the side of the road, too. Both his girls were soft-hearted, but Missy was particularly so, so he drove to her as quickly as he could, knowing how distressing it all had to be for her.

There she was, standing by the side of the road, waving him down as if it would have been possible for him to miss her. He pulled his truck behind her car and quickly climbed out. He expected her to run to him, let him comfort her, tell him exactly what she'd found, and let him dry some of her tears. But she didn't. Missy stayed right by that dog's side. He approached them both and realized that Missy had indeed summed up the dog; the poor thing was a mess.

Missy was crying and trying to tell him something, but all he could really make out was something about some Diane and the F-word which she used about three times. He hated it when she cursed, but she was upset, and given the situation, he couldn't really blame her. He bent down beside her and looked at the dog. Missy was right; she was pregnant. She had scars all over her body, and you could see the old scars and fresh cuts where her legs were still tied. Her face looked the worst though.

He swiftly took out the knife she had instructed him to bring and severed the ropes that tied her legs. The dog moved her head ever so slightly. He weighed his options. They could take this girl back home, but then do what with her? Put some ointment on her? That was ridiculous. Plus, who knew if this dog would be able to survive, and if she did, what kind of baggage would she have? He doubted that a dog that had been through what she had would ever want to snuggle in his lap in front of the fire. He didn't think that either he or Missy would be able to adequately care for this dog, and even if they could, then what? He wasn't interested in another dog, and Missy certainly couldn't afford a dog. He glanced at his watch. It was 8:35. He looked at Missy, who was still looking at the dog, and decided it was time to call a vet clinic. They had to see this shit all the time.

11

the long road home

"Red River Animal Hospital."

"Yeah, good morning. My daughter and I just found a dog alongside 102 about a mile outside town. She's pretty beaten up and when we found her, her legs were tied together. She's alive and has moved her head for us, but that's about it."

"Are you looking for treatment for the animal?"

"I guess I don't know what we're looking for. I don't know if she's going to survive or not, but we're obviously not going to just leave her out here on the side of the road. Have you dealt with situations like this in the past?"

"We've dealt with animals that have been hit by cars or gotten in fights. You can bring the animal in. We can take a look and give you an estimate for treatment."

An estimate? What the hell? "This isn't our dog. We don't want to leave her here, but we're not prepared to pay for treatment." With that, Missy produced a fresh set of tears that he knew was coming but still wasn't prepared for. "Hold on, please," he said and put his hand over the phone. "Missy, this poor girl has been through hell. The best thing we can do is get her someplace where they know what they're doing. You did the right thing by stopping for her. Now we need to pass her along to the folks who can do some good."

He watched Missy stare at the dog, tears rolling down her face, but the sobs that were breaking his heart subsided. He knew her heart was breaking, but he also knew she had a good head on her shoulders. This dog was too much for them to handle, even if they wanted to. She bent down and gave the dog a long kiss on her head. He could see the dog was breathing, but she didn't move. Missy looked up, her eyes heavy with grief and nodded to him.

He got back on the phone. "Thanks for holding. What are our options if we're not willing to pay for treatment?"

"About the only other thing you can do is take her down to the animal shelter. They'll probably put her down, but at least she won't lie there alone and die."

He expressed his gratitude and hung up. In explaining what was about to transpire, Missy melted down as he'd expected, and in all fairness, he didn't like it either. She was sitting by the dog and had moved her head into her lap, stroking the dog's forehead. He marveled at how that could have been the only love that dog ever felt. He was immensely proud of his daughter and the compassionate heart she possessed. He sat down next to her and stroked the dog's head as well. Missy rested her head on his shoulder. He was sure the cars driving down 102 thought they were nuts, but he didn't care. He couldn't remember if he'd ever felt this sad or content at the same time.

Sitting there with her dad, Missy was angry, sad, and hopeless, all at the same time. And she swore while they sat there petting that dog that her breathing was getting stronger and stronger. After about twenty minutes, her dad got up and walked to his truck. He came back with the blanket she'd asked him to bring, and they stretched it out next to the dog. She looked like she weighed about forty pounds—she was real skinny. Missy supported her head and neck, and her dad had the rest. On the count of three, they lifted her as delicately as they could and placed her on the blanket. Missy lovingly folded her into a burrito of sorts, and her dad lifted her off the side of the road. The two of them walked silently back to his truck and placed the dog in the back of the cab.

Her dad spoke first. "Do you need to get to work?" Missy looked at her phone. 9:15. She looked in the back of the cab at the dog she'd just spent more than two hours with.

"I'm probably fired anyway. Diane's such a bitch about stuff that she'd never understand this." She looked at her dad, her long-forgotten mascara still smearing her face. "Can I come with you?"

They drove down the long gravel driveway to the shelter's entrance. Her dad got out of the car, leaving Missy and the dog behind while he went to find out the process for dropping an animal off. Missy sat in the front seat, facing the back seat of the cabin. She spoke softly to the dog, telling her she was a good girl. She reached back and touched the belly of the dog; she could tell her breathing was definitely stronger. She patted the dog a little more assertively, and the dog opened her eyes again. They looked at Missy, but that time they were a little less vacant, Missy was sure of it.

Her dad came out. "They'll put her on a five-day hold. If she survives, and if no one comes forward to claim her, she'll go on the adoption floor. They can't guarantee how long she has after that." He said this with a matter-of-factness that she knew he didn't feel. The words weighed down her body like bricks. Seeing her shoulders fall, he softened a bit. "Baby, I want you to remember that she's safe because of you. Maybe this world has just been too much for her. We're going to take her in here, and I bet whatever happens, she'll remember you kissing her forehead and resting her head in your lap." He paused with his head down. Missy watched him take out his handkerchief and wipe his nose. "Listen, I know this is hard. I get that. But it's time to keep doing the right thing."

Dropping the dog off was agonizing for Missy. Her dad could say whatever he wanted, but after all the hell that sweet girl had lived through, no way was a kiss on the forehead going to be what she took with her if—God forbid—she left this world. She and her dad drove back to her car without saying a word. She sat there after he drove away, looking at the spot where the dog had lain. She'd never felt this kind of grief before. She didn't think she had ever seen anyone suffer like that, and it was the most horrible feeling ever knowing there was nothing she could have done to prevent it, and nothing she could do to take it away. She closed her eyes, breathed deeply, and started the engine. "Just a Dream" by Nelly was on the radio. She turned it off.

She made it home and lay on her bed thinking about kissing the dog's face for the last time as she lay in her blanket burrito on a dirty stainless steel counter. The woman behind the counter waiting to take the dog away had looked at her like she was a crazy person.

She took some more deep breaths to try and relax and buried her face in an old throw pillow. Her face and eyes hurt from the salt in the tears that had been falling all day. Occasionally her phone would ring, but she ignored it. At about one o'clock she looked at her missed calls, and sure enough, three of them were from work. Or what used to be work. She didn't bother listening to the voicemails. She felt guilty for being so selfish, but she just wanted to sleep. It was amazing to her how exhausting emotion could be. She debated between a couch nap and a full-on bed nap, and in the end she put in The Twilight Saga: New Moon, pulled back her covers, and closed the shades. She flipped her pillows to the cool side and drifted off to sleep.

She didn't know how long she'd slept, but when she woke up, there was a fire in her belly that her crappy job in retail had never sparked. Bella. That sweet dog had to be named Bella. Who knew if she would have come up with it had she not fallen asleep to the always-melancholy, human Bella mourning the loss of Edward on her TV, but it seemed like the perfect name for that incredible dog who had been through so much. Why couldn't she go down to the shelter and take Bella's picture and plaster it online? She was on Facebook constantly anyway. If even one or two of her 419 friends were as moved by this sweet girl as she was, well then something had to happen, right?

She jumped out of bed and splashed water on her face. She still looked like shit, but she didn't care. She used her finger to do a quick tooth brushing and went to the same closet where she'd found her keys that morning. It was where she kept her camera. She got in her car and turned the radio back on. This time, "Just the Way You Are" by Bruno Mars was playing. Well, that just seemed fitting.

She got to the shelter a half an hour before they closed. The staff begrudgingly let her in, and she followed their directions down the rows of stalls containing dogs. The smell was horrible. Puppies and dogs were everywhere, barking and begging for her attention. Their eyes searched hers for the possibility that maybe she would be the one that would notice them—and she did. But she knew she had to be there for the dog that she had named Bella. These dogs needed somebody, and she prayed they would get somebody. But Bella needed her.

Missy came around a corner and there she was, pregnant and lying on a wet, concrete floor. She looked cleaner than she had earlier in the day, so that was good. Missy knelt down and tried to mentally implore Bella to remember the morning they'd had and the beautiful bond she thought they had developed. She sat on the filthy floor and looked at Bella. What had that girl lived through, just to make it there to a probable fate that Missy didn't want to think about?

Missy sat there, breathing deeply, marveling at the fact that she'd be able to walk out of that god-forsaken place, but dogs, they wouldn't get to make that decision. She felt foolish and selfish, worrying about whether or not the stench of excrement and death would come out of her clothes. And then she remembered why she was there, and she thought about how much she already loved this precious mom-to-be. It was hard to pin down what she was feeling, so in light of the fact that she'd most certainly lost her job, she wanted to give herself a little time to sit with that sweet dog.

She heard a man clear his throat behind her. She wasn't sure if it was directed at her or not, but she knew the time she longed for was already running out. She just prayed that Bella's wasn't. So she helped in the only way she knew how, by deliberately raising her camera and centering the lens on the heartrending image before her. Slowly, slowly, she began snapping photos.

12

the ups and downs of social media

As 2009 turned into 2010, we found ourselves with a longing for something more. Our post-war, one-and-a-half story on the adorable tree-lined street had served its purpose, but we were ready for the next step. A woman that I worked with told me about the steals that could be gotten on properties south of the Cities. Essentially, a four-bedroom, three-bathroom house in New Market, Minnesota, a charming little community an hour south of Minneapolis, would sell for about the same price as a three-bedroom, one-bathroom house in Minneapolis. And who doesn't want more, just because? It was the four of us—Brian and I, Foster and Jane—and we were still one dog short.

We made several trips to the south metro and loved how crisp, new, and huge those houses were. They had vaulted ceilings over great rooms; big, bright sunny kitchens with gleaming surfaces from top to bottom; and (gasp) dual-vanity master baths. Our current home had a finished loft on the upper level which we loved, but as one of my friends put it, having to go downstairs to use the bathroom was "worse than camping." We went so far as to do a spit-and-polish on our house, and we put it on the market just in time for the Fourth of July weekend, 2010.

A few weeks later, we were with some of our Minneapolis friends— people who make us laugh louder than anyone else in the world—at a barbecue. When we told them of our plans to move to the suburbs, it was like that horrific moment during a conversation in a crowded room when someone decides to drop a choice swear word and all other conversation stops.

We had just told our friend Sara that we listed our house and were going to move about an hour south of the city. At that moment, everyone in the room stopped talking, looked at us, and at least three people said, "Why?" Brian and I looked at each other. We stumbled through our reasons after which our friends pummeled us with questions.

"Do you really want to clean up after three dogs in a 3,500-square-foot house?"

"How's that commute sound when it's thirty below in a blizzard?"

"Ever had any good Indian food in New Market?"

During our cab ride home I thought we'd feel dejected and confused, but we were elated. We didn't want to leave Minneapolis. Sure, those houses were beautiful, but we weren't really "new construction" people anyway. We talked and talked in the twenty minutes it took us to get home and continued to talk for two more hours until we were wound down enough to sleep. This house in this city was our home and always would be. The "For Sale" sign came down that Monday morning, almost three weeks and exactly four showings since it had gone on the market. We started interviewing contractors for our home renovation the Monday after that.

Since leaving the U (which is what everyone in Minnesota calls the University of Minnesota), some of the nurses that I had worked with had been encouraging me to get a Facebook account. I was resistant, in the way that six years earlier I had refused to text. Those were things that "the kids" did, and I was far too hip and comfortable with my stage in life to try and grasp at straws. Well, it turns out I can't live without texting or Facebook, so joke's on me.

Facebook had been a great way for me and everyone else on the planet to reconnect with old friends from high school, arrange quick happy hours with coworkers, or simply regale my 150-and-some-odd friends with whatever "clever" anecdote came into my head. I whittled away hours looking at friends' pictures: their Hawaiian vacation, new 2009 Prius, or the before and after of their kitchen renovation.

But one unexpected obsession I developed occurred after I realized that Facebook was a great way to connect with other animal lovers. There were plenty of people on the planet who loved animals just as much as I did. I was inundated with both heartwarming and heartbreaking stories, and I tried to read them all. Deep, sad, imploring eyes looked back at me from photos of abandoned, abused, and neglected dogs and cats from all over the globe. Some of them were followed by joyous adoption tales, which gave me the hope and desire to keep reading those tragic stories, knowing that at least some would have happy endings.

It was a day in August 2010, and I was perusing the pages of Facebook. As I scrolled through, I came across a photo of a dog with a face as soulful as it was hopeless. She was pictured from the side looking out of a window; it looked like the back of a van. Her brown face and salt-and-pepper muzzle appeared more tar-gray than anything because of all the scars. It looked as though her face and body had been covered in cigarette burns. Before I even started reading her story it broke my heart; it was impossible to imagine what those honey-colored eyes had witnessed. I steeled myself and prepared for what I was about to read.

The words were written by Beth McDuffie, and there will be much more about Beth in the pages to come. These words tell the story of a dog now called Bella and the horrific life she endured and somehow survived at the hands of dogfighters. These words crashed into my soul like a hit and run, only they didn't run. I had no idea that reading these words was going to change me and change my family. It took me three sittings to read them completely, and they caused that kind of chest-heaving cry that should be reserved for mourning the loss of a loved one. And in a way, I suppose I was mourning. This story changed who I was forever when it forced me to realize the depths of depravity of which humans are capable. The following is an excerpt of the story of the dog who is now called Bella, as told by Beth McDuffie:

"My name is Bella, named this by you... at least those of you who worked so very hard to save my life and the lives of my unborn babies. Let me be honest. I was very confused at first about all the fuss over me. I never had that before. I could hear the other dogs talking in the County Shelter where I was waiting to die. They all seemed to be anxious for someone to come along and give them a second chance. When they would ask me about wanting a second chance I would ignore them. I found the best spot I could to lay down and thought about my little babies growing inside me. The floor was hard, but there was food to eat and water to drink, and no one was trying to hurt me, so I laid there waiting. I must admit I sort of hoped my babies would get a chance at life. And hearing the others talk, I sort of hoped they would get one of those rescue things that the others were yapping about. But

I knew my days were numbered and I did not mind so much. I was not afraid to die. In fact, if my babies had to go to the place where I came from... well... there are worse things than death. When you have looked evil in the face you know these things. So I was just sort of waiting and wondering what would become of my babies. Death was finally coming for me. Sometimes when I would lay there and recall the past I would remember the nights I prayed for death. So many nights and so much pain with other dogs being ordered to attack me and hurt me, but always being stopped before they finished the job, and I never blamed the dogs. They were just doing what they were told. Had I been the one ordered to attack, I certainly would have done it. When evil wants you to do something, you do it or you get hurt in ways that angels like you could not understand. That kind of evil cannot live in the heart of someone so kind. I know you are wondering why I did not fight back. So, I guess what that man called a vet saw is the best way to say it. If you look at my legs you will see the scars from the rope where I was tied before being thrown into the "pit." The rope cut very deeply and the scars are bitter reminders of how helpless I was. All I ever really wanted was to be loved, but that was not my life. See, my life was that of a Bait Dog, also known as a Clown Dog. And in my circle, in that world of evil and evil doers, I am not one that is worthy of love. So the scars are bitter reminders of the fact that I was never to be loved and never to be cared for. I would not get a bone to chew on like the fighting dogs that brought the master a lot of money. I was lucky to get a bowl of kibble. I was given just enough to sustain my life. Perhaps had the hunger pains not been so great, I would have had the courage to end it all then. I would have just not eaten. But the hunger was always there and was always so hurtful so I could not refuse the small amount of food I was given. So my pain continued with each auction. Auctions are where the fighting dogs are sold for those who may not know. And the worse they can hurt the bait dog ... and still leave her alive ... the more money they bring. The attacks are very deliberate and are meant to inflict damage that is almost fatal ... but not quite. The bait dog is not allowed the mercy of death. But oh how I prayed for it on many of those nights as the dog would tear at my flesh until I was blinded by my own blood. Then when it was over, when the "hero" was sold, the laughter would begin as they would point to me and talk about what a ferocious girl I was. I was often laying in my own blood and urine. I would defecate uncontrollably and have no choice but to lay there. Any movement before I was allowed and another attack might come. And I forgot to mention: I was always thrown into the pit hog tied with rope like a sacrificial lamb being lead to the slaughter. But that was so I could not escape my fate. On those nights I would think about what my own mother may have had planned for me when I was just a pup. I have no memory of those days, but now, soon to be a mother myself, I can imagine the hopes and dreams she may have had for me. On the nights when it hurt the most, when my ears were ripped and torn, my eyes so filled with blood tears that I could not see, my nose gashed and bleeding into my mouth so I tasted my own blood, my face and my throat torn and bleeding, old scars ripped open and my legs that were already cut from the wire now being bitten and ripped by the teeth of my own kind... on those nights if I thought of what my mother had wanted for me I would pray she never knew how I wet myself when the dog came at me. I hoped she could believe I was in a beautiful place, doing those things that dogs do best... anything but this. And thinking those thoughts about my mother, one night I decided I would fight back. When the vet examined me today, he could only guess that this is what happened. I heard him say the findings on my exam were not so uncommon on Bait Dogs who may have had a little spirit at one time. He speculated that my "spirit" had come after many nights of torture because the evidence of that was fresher than many of my scars. I listened as the man called "Vet" told the woman and man what he thought had happened to me. He told them I am an older girl, and I am. But he told them if they would look very closely they would see that my teeth were not worn down from age. I have no teeth except for my canines and every other one on each side. All of my front teeth are gone. And they were not worn down from age and use. They were pulled. Scars are still in my mouth from the crude home job. At one time "Vet" said that I was most likely a beautiful dog. Pulling my teeth had caused my mouth to look a little strange and had caused me to lose muscle tone in my jaw. But it had insured that I would not hurt one of the money dogs. "Vet" then scared me a little and I cowered as he opened my mouth to look again and to show the woman and man the rest of my humiliation. My canines have been filed down so they could do no damage to the money dogs should I decide to fight back again. "Vet" touched every hurt spot, every scar and showed the woman and man. I thought then they might send me away as I had always thought I was worthless, but I was so worried about my babies and I so hoped that all the strange feelings I had been having all day stayed with me now. All of the humiliation from days passed was nothing compared to this new fear. For the first time in my life I learned of good people and of love in that County Animal Shelter. Oh... it felt so good. While all the others were talking about getting a second chance, I was learning that I might actually get a first chance to be loved, and my babies might have a chance. While I was waiting to die and feeling it was my only way out, I met Dustin and Jessica. They came and took me from the shelter and for the first time I felt love and respect. Whatever came after that did not matter because feeling it once in my life would have been enough. And I met the Woman and Man, Beth and Jerry, at Eagle's Den. Once again there was that wonderful feeling of being loved and respected. There was a gentle touch and food to eat that did not hurt my mouth. There was lotion for my sore legs and clean water. There are other animals too, and they really scared me. I am still very much afraid of other dogs for now, but I know I am safe. But this fear that washed over me when they learned of my shame... I cannot describe it. I thought they would not love me anymore. But instead, the woman took my face in her hands as she had done so many times today and she whispered to me: YOU NEVER HAVE TO BE AFRAID AGAIN. YOU ARE SAFE NOW. And I saw something else. I saw that people can cry too. Jessica cried today when she saw me, and I felt such overwhelming love from her. I learned what it means to have respect from Dustin, her son. When he carried me so gently from his car to Beth's van, I have never been treated so gently and well. And tonight... for the first time in my entire life I am inside a house. I have a nice kennel that is a good place to have my babies when the time comes. There is clean water and a bowl that always has food. The vet told them when these babies are born I will be very skinny so they are giving me vitamins. They have given me my own bed and a soft spot to lay my head and my weary body. They do not let the other dogs near me just now as they know I am afraid. But I have made one friend here that is my kind. Her name is Pee Wee and she is so very tiny. I do not think she will hurt me. I also met a girl named Hope who greeted me when I first arrived. I could tell she was as scared as I was, but she came up to me and licked my face. I wet myself a little and she must have wanted me to feel better about it because she wet herself too. But she told me that she had been through some hard times too, and she said this is a safe spot to land. She told me we can play later, after I have been here for a bit. So I guess that means I am staying and I am getting that first chance. I hope those other guys get their second chance. And I thank all who played a part in giving me this chance I have. I will make the most of it and you will not be sorry. Thank You so much. I am going to need a lot of care in the next few weeks. My babies will be here soon and the Vet said we are going to have to keep a close eye on this as I have not been fed properly and my body is so weak and tired. I cannot ask more of you guys than you have already done because you have given me so much. And my new "Mom and Dad" (I like the sound of that) promised me I will have every chance now and will get what I need."

Quite literally, for days after reading this, I would wake up in the middle of the night, wondering if the horrors of what I had read were happening to an innocent dog at that exact minute. I was so happy Bella was safe, but how many other Bellas were out there? I had always been sickened by the atrocities of dog fighting, but I never even knew this aspect existed. The brutality involved in this blood "sport" overwhelmed me.

And Bella, I couldn't get the sweet face of Bella out of my mind. I saved her sad photo on my phone, I told her heartbreaking story to anyone who would listen, I sent her story to Oprah (foolishly maybe, but she says she's a dog lover) with no response. I had to ask Brian several times to read Bella's story, and he finally did one Saturday afternoon. When he came out of the office, he looked pale. I didn't say anything to him, and he didn't say anything to me until that evening. When he did speak, it wasn't about Bella, so I didn't ask him what effect the story had on him. His silence on the subject told me everything I needed to know.

I was at work the next week, and I called Brian. We were talking about the usual "How's your day going" stuff when suddenly, completely out of the blue, I found myself saying, "What do you think about maybe trying to adopt Bella?" Brian was accustomed to hearing that kind of question. And I was accustomed to hearing the Brains tell me at least four reasons why we weren't going to adopt this dog or that dog whose story had moved me to tears because there had been many of them. None of them had affected me nearly as much as Bella, though, and the same must have been true for Brian because after I asked the question, he paused, just for a few moments.

I couldn't believe my ears when he said, "Well, let's see what we need to do."

13

we look forward to hearing from you

Hello Beth,

Where to start? We know that you're extremely busy, so we'll try and keep this as brief as possible, though there's a lot of info that we want to convey about ourselves and our desire to give Bella her forever home.

My husband Brian and I have been married for twelve years. He's an operations manager for a private investment firm, and I'm a registered nurse. We have two dogs: Foster, our ten-year-old, German Shepherd mix; and Jane, our two-and-a-half-year-old rottie. Both are rescue dogs who had a rough start, but obviously nothing that can compare to sweet Bella. Both are well socialized and dog-friendly. We live in a great neighborhood called Columbia Park in Northeast Minneapolis, Minnesota.

We try and provide Foster and Jane with the very best food and care that we can. Foster eats Innova brand food, and Jane eats Innova Light. (We ladies don't keep the pounds off as well as the guys!) Among the positives that we can provide for Bella is that we never kennel or board our pets; rather, we have a licensed and bonded pet-sitter who comes and stays in our home if we are traveling. We also have an in-home veterinarian named Dr. Ann Fisher who comes to our house to do routine check-ups, labs, basic diagnostics, etc. If they need more comprehensive work done, Dr. Fisher does work out of a clinic as well. I cannot stress enough that no expense is spared when it comes to the health of our pets. We consider their well-being as important, if not more important, than our own. My husband is an avid dog-walker, so they both get at least two walks a day, and Jane enjoys going to doggie day care and the dog park, so they do get out of the house! Foster is sort of the elder statesman and would rather take a nap.

Why do we want Bella? We both feel that when we look into an animal's eyes, we're moved. There's such purity there. When we look into Bella's eyes in her photos and video, we're actually shaken. She's got such strength, soul, courage, and grace, and despite enduring the very worst that life can offer, she's maintained that purity as well. Now, we'd like to give her the very best that life can offer. I'm not sure if having large dogs makes this a deal-breaker for us, but like I said, if we're lucky enough to be considered, we'd be committed to doing WHATEVER we have to in order to make the transition into our home successful for everyone involved. We've had to do lots of work with our other dogs, especially Foster, and we've been rewarded 100-fold. This doesn't scare us—we welcome the opportunity.

As far as obtaining Bella, should we be lucky enough to get to that point, our thought is we would drive to NC with Foster and Jane to do a meet-and-greet on Bella's territory. We hope that doesn't sound presumptuous. There are probably countless families that are waiting to adopt Bella. We just want you to know that we're taking this very seriously.

No words can tell you how grateful we are for the work that you do. Thanks in advance for considering us as Bella's forever family. We look forward to hearing from you.

Best wishes and very kind regards,
Cynthia Schlichting and Brian Carlson (and Foster and Jane)

That was the e-mail we sent to Beth McDuffie at Eagle's Den Rescue on September 13, 2010. We didn't know much about Eagle's Den yet, other than they had given beautiful words to a beautiful girl that we wanted to call ours. The fact that Brian had agreed to try and bring Bella into our home was enough to excite me, which could potentially be as big of a negative as a positive.

With the Brains on board, it was impossible not to envision her racing around the back yard, sleeping in the guest room, waiting for a treat in the kitchen, or finding her favorite place to look out the window. But how much rehabbing would she need? Had the horrors that she had suffered for who knows how long done irreparable damage? Would Foster and Jane indeed be a deal breaker for us, or could they be useful in helping this damaged girl adapt to life in our home? If God's plan did include welcoming the beautiful Bella into our home, how would it time out with both our home renovations, which were solidly in the planning phase, and the arrival of Bella's litter of nine precious pups, which were delivered with Beth's help the day after Labor Day? I had to take a step back and remind myself that I have a habit of getting ahead of myself, a habit which has caused me huge disappointment on more than one occasion. Then, unexpectedly on September 14, we received this response:

Hello Cynthia, Brian, Foster & Jane,

I wanted to assure you that your request to adopt Bella has been received and you will certainly be considered.

I tend to read the applications and requests in the order I receive them and sort them based on a gut feeling. It has not failed me yet. I am very impressed with what you have said and wanted to assure you that your application is most definitely at the top of my list right now. I still have to check references, but your words ring true and sincere, and that means a lot.

I will be back in touch with you soon, after I have had a chance to do reference checks.

Thank you, and thank you for the love and care you so obviously devote to the wonderful souls entrusted to your care. I honestly believe animals choose us rather than the other way around and that "gut" feeling is what we MUST rely on so often.

Beth & Jerry
AND BELLA & PACK

We were pleased to have gotten a response so quickly, but what did this mean? We were at the top of the list, but how long was the list? In the time it took her to check references, was the absolutely perfect family—even more perfect than I thought our family was for her—going to swoop in and take this girl from us, the girl that we'd already grown attached to? Additionally, this just made my Facebook addiction even worse. I was constantly on Eagle's Den's page, eagerly looking for photos and updates on Bella and her newborn pups.

Tragically, the updates started coming in. And they were heartbreaking. One by one, Bella's puppies were dying, more innocent victims of the attacks that Bella suffered as a bait dog. Her injuries were new, and her precious pups all suffered brain damage due to the trauma Bella experienced when she was attacked while pregnant. They were unable to nurse and unable to walk. According to Beth, this amazing girl who had suffered horrors that most of us don't even want to imagine seemed to sense which one was going to pass next. Beth said she watched with dread as Bella would pull the next little one close to her, and every time that puppy would be gone shortly after. The pain and anguish were evident on Bella's scarred face. Seven of her nine precious puppies were gone within a week, leaving two.

Beth named the remaining two pups "Dusty" and "Jesse" after the wonderful mother and son team that had driven her from the Westerfield, South Carolina, shelter to Beth and Jerry at Eagle's Den after pictures of her began circulating on Facebook. I don't even know how many people were responsible for Bella's rescue, but I know it was many. Jessica and Dustin arrived at Westerfield at seven o'clock in the morning, and Brian and I found out later through Beth that if they had arrived at 7:15, Bella would have been gone. She had been granted several pardons based on interest and the number of people that were trying to help her, but her time was up. Jessica and Dustin had to be there no later than 7:00 a.m., or Bella would have been euthanized. There were so many pieces that had to come together in her rescue, and thank God the appropriate players came into place. But sadly, the outcomes for their namesakes were no brighter than for Bella's other precious pups. Despite the constant care from Beth and Jerry and the many prayers and well-wishes from Bella's supporters, Dusty succumbed next. There were high hopes for Jesse's survival, but I'm sorry to report that sweet Jesse passed away three weeks after birth, her eyes open, but still unable to walk.

As I found out about the passing of each of Bella's babies, the break in my heart for her grew bigger. Bella had obviously had many litters in her life. How many of them were hers and hers alone, to love, nurture, and cherish? And with the last chance she had, all of her puppies were taken from her—one last, fatal insult from the monsters that had already brought immeasurable suffering to this beautiful girl.

At one point, when I found out about the passing of another pup, I was at work and the tragedy of it all struck me at once. I went into the bathroom and sat on the sink. And I cried like I was in the privacy of my home. I cried like nothing was ever going to be right in the world again. I cried like I hadn't cried since I read Bella's story. And I can't remember when I'd cried like that before. If Beth and Jerry did in fact find a home that suited Bella better, I would be so happy for that incredibly lucky family. If she were destined to be our girl, though, then Bella wasn't going to want for anything. The rest of her days with us would be filled with warm beds, neck scratches, ear rubs, a full belly, and more kisses than she could possibly want. I didn't care how damaged that dog was, or how much time, money, blood, sweat, or tears we would have to put into her rehabilitation. If Bella was going to be our girl, we would spend all her remaining days assuring her she was loved, safe, and home forever.

As it turned out, two orphans named Hans Solo and Jedi arrived at Eagle's Den shortly before Jesse's tragic passing, desperately needing milk and someone to love and care for them. Bella with her huge heart took them in, nursed them, cleaned them, and loved them like they were her own. Thanks to Bella, Hans Solo and Jedi were soon adopted out into their forever homes. Beth said they looked just like Bella's little tan pups.

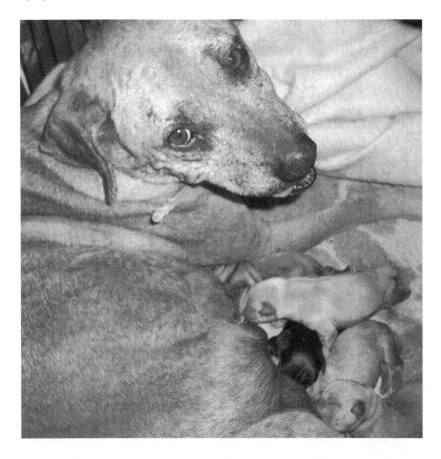

The first five of Bella's pups, shortly after birth. Beth had high hopes since they looked so plump and healthy.

14

bless you for loving bella

September 18, 2010
Cynthia, Brian, Foster and Jane:

After doing our usual checks, and checking with your vet... we still are waiting to hear from your last reference. (We had trouble with our phone and computer yesterday... STORMS!!! Country living is great... but it does shut us down sometimes.)

However, I believe I told you that my intuition plays a huge role in my decision making. I see no point in waiting for the last reference to come in. When I ran my usual "checks" for you guys... you passed with flying colors. I will, of course use the reference I receive for your file, but Jerry and I went through all applications and the checks we made and you guys were our favorites. Bella liked you best too. We asked her and she said she would like to have Foster and Jane as her forever siblings as well as you two as her parents.

The little ones she adopted will not be a problem as they are older and will be finished nursing in about two weeks.

So... I wanted to get word to you quickly that we really liked your family for Bella. We have a little time to work out the details. I know you said you planned to drive to get her.

I do apologize profusely if I have been a little off in my communication. Even though my brain remains sharp with MS... it does not always come out that way. But I have all the forms in front of me today where my husband and my favorite volunteer, Kelly, did the checks for me and it looks wonderful. We are thrilled that Bella will be joining your family.

Beth & Jerry
Beth McDuffie, co-Founder and Assoc. Director
Eagle's Den Animal Haven & Rescue

September 19, 2010
Dear Beth,

Speechless....my hands are shaking as I type this email. Brian and I are overwhelmed, honored, excited, and nervous about being chosen to give Bella her forever home. I'd like to say this is going to be a short email, but we've got lots of questions for you. We just want to make sure we're 1,000 percent prepared and ready to give Bella and the rest of the family the happiest home that we can. My mind is going 100 miles a second, so if this seems really scattered, I apologize!!

How big is Bella? How is her temperament? Like I said, both Foster and Jane came from less-than-favorable conditions, but we have no experience adopting a dog that came from Bella's background. For example, Foster and Jane love to wrestle and play with each other, and when they're doing this, they may sound like some of the horrific experiences that Bella has witnessed. Will she be able to tell from their energy that playing is an enjoyable thing and not something to fear? If she does relapse and forget the happy place that she is in now, how do we redirect her and remind her that she's safe? Also, when Foster and Jane "guard-dog" (bark at the mail man, etc.), they definitely sound more vocal, though none of this is ever directed at each other. One concern is that Jane is your typical two-and-a-half-year-old with energy to match. You'd be hard-pressed to find a sweeter dog on the planet, but when she gets excited, she does get "mouthy." This is usually when Foster and Jane are sharing guard dog duties, and she'll lightly nip at Foster. Her intention is never to harm him, and she never has; she just gets caught up in the moment sometimes.

One of the reasons that we've been talking about adopting a third dog is that we're doing extensive renovations to our house which will give us more space. We're hoping that everything will be near completion by Thanksgiving, which we're hoping would time out well with the weaning of Hans Solo and Jedi. It would also be easiest for us to get time off of work to make the trek from Minnesota to NC. We've mapped out how we'd get there, and we think we'll need to rent an RV in order to give everyone enough room. (If you knew us, you'd know how hilarious the notion of this is, but anything for Bella!) It's about a twenty-two-hour drive, so we'd need to take a couple of days to get down there and a couple of days to get back. Does this time frame seem reasonable?

We're not sure how Bella's confidence level is, but do you think obedience training would be good for her? Also, what about discipline? Obviously, we never physically discipline our dogs, but will she be OK with verbal correction? Or maybe she'll just never do anything naughty! :)

What type of food will be best for her to eat? Will she be healthy and strong enough to be spayed? We're completing our lower level and would ideally like to give Bella a room down there. Does she do OK with stairs? If not, we can make room on the main level. Also, does she sleep in a kennel? We have a huge kennel that Jane used to use that would work well for her; otherwise, we'll keep her in a room with the door closed if we're not home. This is what we do with Foster and Jane as well—less potential for trouble! Do you think she'll suffer from separation anxiety? Brian works about forty-five hours a week, and I work anywhere from thirty-two to forty. Will this be OK for her?

Finally, can you suggest any resources that would help us in preparing to bring Bella home? We've read a lot about the Vick dogs, but is there anything else you can suggest that would make us more informed about Bella and how to care for her?

OK, I'm SO sorry this is so long. I can't even imagine how busy you are, so hopefully this isn't a huge frustration for you! Please don't take these questions as reservations, rather as our commitment to Bella that we're going to take the best possible care that we can of her. Our goal is that she, Foster, and Jane don't have even a second of unhappiness with us. Thank you so, so much, and please be generous in the kisses that you give the entire pack from us, especially of course, sweet Bella.

All of our very best,

Cindy, Brian, Foster, and Jane (Bella's family—we like the sound of that!)

September 20, 2010

Hi Cynthia & Brian

I just wanted to acknowledge that I received this email and also that the final reference has arrived. As I stated before, you are absolutely the best choice for Bella.

I will sit down tomorrow and cover all of your questions. Please, ask anything you need to know. With so many coming in and going out, and Jerry and I both always falling in love with each and every one, we always have to rely on you guys to ask questions.

She is laying by my chair snoring now. I am very happy to report that she is not so emaciated now. She is eating well, and her skin is looking so much better. I know it feels better to her. I just did not know how recent some of her injuries were.

Bless you for loving Bella... it takes very special people to love and want to understand a dog who has been through so much. As I read this email, the one thing that I kept thinking about was my first bait dog that I adopted. And so many since... you will never know the kind of love these dogs give from another. Not to take anything away from any dog, because each one is special in their own right and makes their own special spot in your heart... but a dog that has been used as bait or a "clown" as they are more commonly called around here, really appreciates everything so much and it shows. I KNOW they never forget where they have been. But I also KNOW that they love and give so much deeper because of what they have suffered. They simply do not matter in the lives they live and the world they live in. They DO NOT EXIST except to be hurt by the loved and cherished, popular dogs. They may even be used to breed, but if they ever fight back then their teeth are ground down or pulled so they cannot hurt the "prize." They are given enough food to keep them alive, but are easily replaced if and when they die. No one sheds a tear. Their fear is evident night after night and day after day ... and if they are unfortunate enough to become a mother, their babies will be quickly snatched from them if they look like good Pits and can be used. Many times though, as with Bella, they continue to use the dog and it is less trouble for them to get rid of the dog, pups and all. And the pups suffer the fate we saw with Bella. I have no doubt she has been there before and they kept her each time.

Just imagine how Bella feels now having food brought to her on a regular basis, her water always clean and her sweet face washed with a soft cloth before we apply Vitamin E and rub her coat and skin down. We also make sure she knows where Hans Solo and Jedi are at every moment. All talk is gentle and she is given treats and has her own toys and bed. She is nurtured, as she will be by you. And what she feels will not be gratitude... it goes much deeper than that. She will feel respected and worthy and will give it back tenfold. All of her life she has felt worthless, unloved and frankly... as a non being. To not only be treated as a life but with respect and love... and to have needs met that others took for granted... WOW... can you imagine? It will take her about a week to understand when she gets to you that you have taken her because you WANT her and because you LOVE her. She will sense that you are good people right away. And the adjustment to your Foster and Jane will take a little time. Just let them make friends in their own space and time... and take it slowly. (I hope what I am about to say does not offend you because it is meant as a huge compliment!) But from the impression and gut feeling I get from you, as well as your references... you have the heart and spirit of a true warm-bloodied animal. Bella will know this. And it will not take her long to attach herself to one of you. She will love you both, but she will choose one as her "Pack Leader." And there is no greater compliment that a dog can give than to accept you as the leader of their pack... it means total trust... and Bella will feel a part of that pack for the first time in her life. She will know she belongs and that will make her heal and make her whole. She will love the other just as much... and that one will be a play mate of sorts. Bait dogs always do this. Most dogs do, but Bait dogs seem to have a special bond with people they accept.

I better end this now or I will go on forever and have not answered any of your questions... I will save it for tomorrow. The one thing I can absolutely advise is that you treat Bella the same as you do the others... the same love and respect... no more or no less... and give her time and space to adjust. You will be amazed how quickly it happens and how close this wonderful dog will get to you both. For her, it is all about being treated as though she is a living, breathing being... and with respect. Being treated normally in other words. Normal is far above special for her. Something tells me you have the ability to stand in Bella's "booties" and walk a mile on her life path. So you will have no problems... Once you look into her eyes, and she looks into yours, and your souls meet for the first time... there will be no turning back. That is when your hearts and spirits will truly unite and you will be able to sit down and tell anyone what Bella thinks on any given day. And you will be able to do that because she will see in you the same thing I felt when I read your words. And she will allow you in. When you look in her eyes you will see what she has seen and she will see what you are offering her... It is the most remarkable experience I have ever had... the first time I "met" and accepted a Bait Dog.

Rest Well... and I have told Bella all about her family... I talk to her about her new siblings, Foster and Jane ... and her Mom and Dad as I rub her legs with the oils we are using to help the scarring and itching. Her eyes are a bit softer now. I will send you pics tomorrow.
Beth & Jerry
Beth McDuffie, co-Founder and Assoc. Director
Eagle's Den Animal Haven & Rescue

And with that e-mail, Beth all but alleviated our fears. Bella would be our girl, and we would make it work. We would give her time, we would give her respect, and most importantly, we would give her love. We knew once she was here, she was here forever, regardless of how difficult her incorporation into our family would be. To say we weren't nervous would be a total lie, but our excitement overrode our anxiety, and the planning for our trip to North Carolina began.

15

you ready?

Have you ever nervously waited and waited for something you've planned for, for what seems like forever, and then right before it happens you're more calm and cool than you had been since the whole thing started? Well, that's not what happened as we prepared ourselves to make the trip to North Carolina the day before Thanksgiving.

The two months spent preparing for this day had been a whirlwind. Our renovations that were supposed to be finished around Thanksgiving had (of course) not even been started. I'm sure that anyone who has done any significant home improvement is unfazed by that news. We had been feverishly trying to find a place to live for the four to eight weeks that it would take to finish the project, and another thing you may be unfazed to hear is that finding short-term housing for yourself, your husband, your German Shepherd, your Rottweiler, and your Pit bull-mix was surprisingly difficult. We spent hours poring over websites, Craigslist, and newspaper ads until Brian had the brilliant idea of contacting our beloved realtor. Perhaps she had a trick or two up her very experienced sleeve that could help us out of this bind.

Well, Sherri continued to be a blessing to us because she did, in fact, have a couple who had moved and had been trying to sell their home for months with no luck. It was about a mile from where we currently lived, and it was another one-and-a-half story with a huge fenced yard. Oh, and they didn't mind dogs. We were ecstatic and couldn't believe our good fortune, so we sent Sherri a check, just as a little token of our appreciation. In true Sherri form, she never cashed it.

Coordinating our trip to North Carolina had also proven challenging. Our intended plan of renting an RV and piling all of us into it to drive halfway across the country to pick up Bella was simply too impractical. Fueling those things was ridiculously expensive, and the thought of driving it through Chicago during rush hour was horrifying. I think what sealed it for us, though, was the fact that the closest either one of us had ever come to camping were the crappy hostels we had stayed at in Europe. The maintenance that came along with renting an RV was, let's just say, intimidating. (You want us to do WHAT with the toilet?) We needed a Plan B. We considered flying down and driving back up, but the cost of renting a car one-way was proving to be a bit prohibitive. We hated the thought, but we contacted Beth about flying round-trip to bring Bella back home with us.

Luckily, Beth thought it would be fine. She said Bella had never really displayed any fear toward loud noises, and while she was sure the experience wouldn't be pleasant for Bella, Beth thought that she would recover from it quickly. We made the tough decision to fly down and pick up our girl and then trust the airline to deliver her safely back to Minnesota, a trip that included a two-hour layover in Atlanta. We didn't like it, but it was our best choice.

Many, many people had been touched by Bella's story just as Brian and I had, and for that reason I made many friends on Facebook that were almost as excited about Bella's journey home as we were. As I posted updates about purchasing her matching leash and collar set, her adorable winter coat (she was from the south, after all), and the kennel that would be used to transport her to us, the excitement grew among the group.

Then, on Wednesday, November 24, 2010, our alarm went off at five in the morning. Brian and I woke, sat up in bed, and looked at each other. This was it. This was the day that we were going to get Bella. Tomorrow evening we'd be home, and we would now be responsible for three precious lives. It was up to us to give them a happy, safe, comfortable, and harmonious home. Were we up to the task? Obviously we'd given our decision to bring Bella into our home a tremendous amount of thought and consideration, but with the unknown there is always a "what if."

Before we got up to begin our journey, Brian looked at me and said, "You ready?"

All I said was, "Yep." I had butterflies in my stomach, and the cup of coffee that I slammed on the way to the airport didn't help. But after enjoying both the body scanner AND a pat-down (you're welcome, TSA), we made our way to the gate that was taking us to Fayetteville, NC, and a sweet, scarred, and damaged-but-not-destroyed little girl named Bella. We knew our lives would be changed. But we sure didn't know how much.

16

the day before thanksgiving

Fayetteville, NC, is home to Fort Bragg Army Base, the first miniature golf course in the country, and it also is apparently a three-time winner of the National Civic League's prestigious "All-American City" Award, more than any other city in North Carolina. It also has a teeny, tiny airport, and that's where we landed, rented a car, and made our way to Lumberton, North Carolina. Beth had decided it was best for us not to make the trip all the way to Eagle's Den because of road construction that was making navigation in the area difficult even for those familiar with it. So she, Jerry, and Bella would meet us at a local restaurant, and we'd finally, FINALLY get to meet the girl that we'd fallen head-over-heels for months earlier.

Making the drive through the picturesque countryside seemed almost eerie. We took in the North Carolina sunshine, snapped happy photos of each other, and listened to the CDs that we'd made to commemorate the occasion. (We titled them "Bella Roadtrip #1" and "Bella Roadtrip #2." Yep, we were just as creative as we had been on "Dog Day.") For all practical purposes, this was a perfect day. When Brian and I spoke of it later, though, we shared a common thought. Despite the rolling hills, gorgeous trees, and abundant sunshine, there was an almost sinister quality that hung in the air. I'm not sure what it was, but it was something that we both felt.

We had been texting and calling Beth to let her know of our progress, and as we pulled onto the exit that would take us to the parking lot where Beth, Jerry, and Bella were waiting for us, the adrenaline began pulsing through my body. I felt like I could run to that parking lot faster than we were driving. I'm sure I was flushed, and I was sitting as far forward as I could, straining to get the first glimpse of the dog that we had cried for, prayed for, and hoped for—the girl that we missed desperately even though we had yet to meet her. We made the final turn in our rented Chevy Impala, and I swear it was like seeing celebrities, only better.

We got out of the car, and about thirty feet in front of us were two of the most unassuming people I've ever seen. Beth's long, silver hair was pulled back in a loose ponytail. She was wearing a yellow pantsuit the exact color of buttercream frosting. Jerry had on cream-colored pants with a red flannel shirt. Both had the weathered hands and faces of people who worked very hard for something that they cared about deeply. I don't think I've ever looked into kinder eyes.

And then there was Bella. Beth and Jerry walked toward us, and Bella walked in between them. She was scarred, that's for sure, but her coat, which had once appeared almost tar-gray, had returned to a pretty brown. She looked so much better than she did in the initial photos and video that we had seen. Her belly still hung low and swollen from her previous litters, including her precious litter of nine that were lost. She came up almost to Beth's knees and looked so tiny and fragile to me.

After the months spent anticipating our adoption, the moment was here. It was dreamlike, and I wasn't sure what to expect. Had Bella, in fact, felt our love over the miles? Did she know that Brian and I were there to take her the 1,271 miles (according to Google Maps) back to Minneapolis and her forever home? Did she know that a very exuberant Jane and very grumpy Foster were going to be her new brother and sister? Did she know that no matter what happened, we were going to love, protect, and cherish her forever? Well, she must not have because as they drew closer, Bella began to hesitate. Not a lot, but enough that we could tell that Bella loved Beth and Jerry, that she felt safe with them. And we were new, and new people were scary.

We shook hands and hugged and then both Brian and I bent down and met Bella for the very first time. I'll never forget how her eyes looked. You know how when you get to know someone their appearance changes? How an endearing personality can make someone that much more attractive, and how that works conversely with someone not so wonderful? Bella looks exactly the same to me today as she did that first moment we met. I could tell in that first fleeting second that Bella had a heart and a soul as open and pure as any that I've ever met—not to take away from Foster or Jane. I hope it's clear that the love I feel for them is monumental, but something happened when Brian and I looked at Bella. Most could not have survived the atrocities that Bella had endured. She had survived for a reason, and that reason was to come into our lives and enrich it beyond our wildest dreams. Or was there something more?

Beth and Jerry wanted to go into the restaurant and grab a quick bite, get to know us in person a little bit, and answer any additional questions we had about our Bella. We made Bella comfortable in their van, and the four of us made our way inside. "Table for four?" Yes, please.

Sitting across from Beth and Jerry in that unpretentious restaurant was surprisingly eye-opening. Not only were these two tireless in the world of animal rescue, but they were also passionate advocates for exploited children. They had a world of experience between the two of them, and we marveled at some of the stories they shared with us. So we sat and we ate, and it became obvious that parting with Bella was going to be more difficult for Beth and Jerry than we had imagined.

Jerry had his plate of food and had meticulously set up a stack of napkins beside it. Every once in a while he'd take a morsel of food and place it on top of those napkins. He'd look at Beth and mumble, "For

Bella." He closely examined this piece of meat and that one to make sure it would be easy enough for Bella to eat because her teeth had been pulled. Eventually, our meal began winding down, and I realized just how excited I was to begin our lives with Bella.

The conversation turned exclusively to Bella, and we told them about the house we'd be renting during the renovations, how we planned for Bella to sleep with us until she settled into her life with us, that she would be eating "California Natural" food because the guy at the pet food store had assured us it was like chicken noodle soup for a sensitive puppy tummy. Beth approved. After much protest from them, Brian and I paid the tab, and we made our way back to Beth and Jerry's van.

There was the face that I already loved looking out the back window at us. They opened the door and gently helped her out. Jerry spread out the feast he had brought for her and Bella ate every little bit, in doggie heaven the whole time. Then, the time came. I knelt down and took off the collar that Bella had worn during her time at Eagle's Den and replaced it with the little purple collar with paw prints that we had bought for her. We attached her matching leash and stood up. Beth had us begin walking to our car, and for a short while, she and Jerry walked with us. She then touched me on the shoulder and said, "Here's where we should leave."

I hugged her and Jerry, and Brian shook their hands. In those last seconds, we tried to convey the depth of our gratitude, not just for the love and care they had given to Bella, but for the love and care that they gave all the dogs that were in their care. They took in dogs that everyone else would have given up on, and they literally worked miracles. And we were about to take one of those miracles home with us.

Beth and Jerry bent down and kissed Bella. Jerry gave her a lingering hug, and the tears made his kind eyes shine. We parted ways, and Beth and Jerry slipped away so fast that Bella didn't notice they were gone until the van was driving out of the parking lot. She turned and watched it go, and I'm sure that her heart cried for them.

Brian drove and I sat in the backseat with Bella. She sat up right beside me. I had to text a few people just to let them know that we had her, and everything was wonderful. She spent a great deal of her time sizing me up as we made our way to the hotel where we'd be spending the night. She'd look at me with eyes that, because of the light, were the same color as maple syrup. And they were maybe the most beautiful eyes I had ever seen. Brian and I spoke to her, told her how pretty she was, and told her how much we loved her probably a hundred times by the time we reached our hotel.

Getting Bella into the car had really been no problem, but getting Bella out of the car and into the hotel was no small feat. She was absolutely terrified of everything. Brian helped by lifting her out of the car, but then she was incredibly skittish, sniffing as she walked around.

A somber farewell to Beth and Jerry, who helped her heal.

Not one hundred percent sold on us...yet.

The slightest noise would cause her to crouch down as though she were avoiding who knows what, and forget about her tail—it was tucked tightly between her legs. Her eyes were huge, fearful, and heartbreaking. I'm sure I'll use those words to describe her eyes often as I tell you her story. We got to the double doors that led into the hotel, and Bella pancaked down, all four legs just collapsing under the oppressive fear she was experiencing. Brian again picked her up and carried her through the doors, an act that he would be required to do many, many times during our stay.

We made it to the front desk, and Bella was obviously traumatized. We explained our situation to the attendant, and they were as sensitive as they could be. The only dog-friendly rooms were on the fourth floor. ("You can just take the elevator up that's right around the corner.") OK, so the first snafu occurred when we walked around that corner to an open room that appeared to be some sort of decrepit conference room. Propped up across the room and in direct view of Bella was an enormous mirror, so as she came around the corner, the first thing she saw was her own reflection. Pancake. I quickly shut the door to the conference room, and both Brian and I bent down to try and gently reassure her that she was safe. For the moment it appeared we had been marginally successful.

We stood up and made our way to the elevator. It looked and sounded like it was from the 1940s because as soon as we pressed the button, it made this incredibly loud churning noise that only got louder as it got closer. Pancake. We tried to coax her onto the elevator once it arrived, but Bella absolutely refused. We tried the stairway, which was right next to the elevator, but, if anything, that was worse. Simply opening the door to the stairwell sent her into a panic. So again, Brian had to physically lift her on and off of the elevator. By the time we arrived on the fourth floor, I think everyone was already exhausted.

We made it to our room, threw our luggage on the bed, and sat on the floor—not something we normally do on carpet that we don't own, but we wanted some face time with our adorable and scared girl. Her demeanor changed dramatically. She was willing to get close and really look us in the eyes. We had an absolute ball kissing her on her little forehead groove, and telling her what a good girl she was and how excited her brother and sister (well, sister anyway) were to meet her.

Because of the horrible condition of her skin when she arrived at Eagle's Den, Beth and Jerry had been putting on various kinds of ointments to help her heal. Her coat looked 100 percent better than it had in the initial photos, which was wonderful. It had left her feeling pretty grimy, though. We had brought some dog wipes from home, just in case, and both Brian and I grabbed a handful and started wiping her down. It helped a little but not a lot. We sat for a while longer, watched a little TV, and marveled that we were finally there.

And then Brian said, "Should we try and give her a bath?" This would prove to be the first of many lessons we were going to learn.

We took the plastic bag out of the garbage can by the bed and filled the can with water. Our room had only a shower, so using the can as a bucket would make it easier to direct the water on her and would hopefully be a lot less intimidating for her than a jet stream of water coming at her from the wall. We sat on the floor in the tiny bathroom (ick) and tried to coax Bella to come in. She sat outside the door and looked at us, her eyes filled with dread. We considered aborting the mission, but as we discussed it, we thought that this may be a good first attempt at bonding. If we placed her in a situation that she perceived as scary, and she saw that everything was OK and that she was safe, maybe it would help her build some trust in us. Things had been going along well up until this point, but a lot was at stake here.

One of our rules had been that Bella wouldn't have even a moment of unhappiness with us, and right then she clearly wasn't thrilled. The last thing that we wanted was for her to be afraid, or think that our intentions were anything but the absolute best for her, but there were probably going to be many things in the future that would cause her a great deal of fear. We decided that this opportunity was as good as any to show our girl that even though the hands in her past had been cruel, going forward, all she would know was a kind, soft, loving touch.

So we tried for a while longer to get Bella into the bathroom on her own accord. What we didn't know was that in addition to a lack of trust in us, Bella also had a paralyzing fear of small spaces. Brian rose and walked towards her to again lift her up and bring her into the shower. Bella's entire body seemed to shrink as she looked up at him, terrified. He spoke gently to her as he walked, and he kissed her on the forehead before he picked her up. What I saw next was something that I would see often, and its effect on me would always be the same.

The fear completely left Bella's face as Brian lifted her off the ground, but that wasn't a good thing. As he walked by, her face was almost parallel with mine. And her face was empty—that's the only word that fit. Bella wasn't there. I thought the lump in my throat might kill me. Brian was carrying her and couldn't see it, and unless you see it, you can't describe it. He set her gently in the shower and I forced my-self not to cry. It took absolutely everything I had. We spoke gently to her, poured the warm water over her coat and massaged the shampoo into her fur. During her bath, she didn't come back to us. I knew a little about dog-fighting, and I knew that before fights it's very common for the "men" to take the opposing fighter and wash it to make sure there was no poison or anything else that could otherwise affect the fight. Perhaps this had happened to Bella in the past. Who knows what hap-pened to Bella in the past? All I knew was that we'd already broken our promise to her. My heart broke into I-don't-know-how-many pieces as we helped her out of the shower.

We brought her out of the bathroom after she'd done the standard full body shake and began drying her off. Just like that, her demeanor changed again. Bella came back. She looked into our eyes and allowed us to coo at her and love her. From that one bath her coat felt better. We got her as dry as we could with the thin hotel towels, and then she went to lie down on the adorable pink blanket that one of the Eagle's Den volunteers had so kindly made for her. We sat on the floor and watched her sleep. We couldn't believe we were sitting in the same room with Bella. We couldn't believe that it was now up to us to read her fears and gain her trust. And we couldn't believe how beautiful she was.

We took her downstairs to go outside three more times before we turned in for the evening, and each time the lobby was a little busier. Bella was distressed enough from the elevator, but each time we encountered a group of people, you guessed it—pancake. And for the most part, rather than looking at her with concern, most looked at her with more distaste than I've ever seen. But there was a table that had what looked like a grandmother and her four grandkids sitting at it. The little ones were the only ones that looked excited and screamed "Puppy!" at their grandma when they saw our terrified little girl. Grandma looked at Bella and gave her a sad smile. I think she'd seen Bellas in the past, and I think it made her very, very sad.

Between Bella's fear and our frustration with the growing number of insensitive people in the hotel lobby, we decided that after our 10:30 trip downstairs, Bella was done for the night. She'd taken care of business each time we'd taken her out, and we'd also brought along a copious amount of puppy pads in case of accidents. We spread those out across the room, and told Bella she was in for the night. She'd definitely paid her dues. We turned on the TV and Brian and I propped up the pillows and breathed a sigh of relief. We hadn't pushed our poor girl off the deep end yet.

We called to her, and to our surprise she hopped right up on the bed and took her place in between us. The relief and joy that that simple action gave us both is something I'll never forget. She took her place in between us, and we absent-mindedly stroked her fur while we spoke softly about the day. Before we knew it, she began snoring, and I mean it when I say that it was one of the most beautiful sounds I'd ever heard. Now we were free to move on to our next concern; have I mentioned yet that the airline doesn't allow animals to be transported to a destination if the forecasted low temperature is less than 10 degrees? The Thanksgiving forecast for Minneapolis? High 18, low 9.

I had told friends and family about this, and we were getting frantic e-mails, texts, and Facebook updates wanting to know our plans. Over the past three years or so, we had been using an absolutely wonderful woman named Pat to come to our home and dog-sit Foster and Jane. We'd tried to kennel Foster a few times, but it was just too hard on him. We found Pat and never strayed from her. But with the holiday, Pat was available for only one night. She needed to leave by noon in order to make Thanksgiving dinner with her family who lived three hours away. One of us had to get home.

So we had devised a plan that would allow us all to fly to Atlanta, and if in fact Bella was unable to get to Minnesota, then Brian would book a flight to Chicago, and he and Bella would stay at the Hilton directly attached to O'Hare. We'd confirmed with the airline that there was room for both of them on the flight and booked the room. I'd make it home to Foster and Jane by 8 p.m., and Brian and Bella would join us there on Friday. The forecast low was a balmy 13. In case of emergency, we were ready. We watched Letterman for a little while and then turned off the lights. Bella's snores helped us drift off to sleep.

Considering the full day we'd all had, everyone enjoyed a quiet night and slept soundly. We woke up the next morning with Bella still sleeping in between us; she hadn't moved from that spot all night. Incredibly, Bella had no accidents in the hotel room overnight, but that increased the urgency to make the pilgrimage back outside to see if she needed to go potty. Again, Brian had to lift her on and off the elevator, and as we got down to the main floor, we were relieved to see the rest of the hotel appeared to be sleeping; even the front desk was empty. She went out the double doors on her own, but it was obvious that she didn't love the idea. Her tail was again glued between her legs, and she didn't completely pancake, but she walked crouched close to the ground, indicating that she was still mistrustful of her surroundings.

By the time we had gotten all of our things packed and ready to go, other hotel guests had started to stir. We sat on the floor with Bella and dreaded this next step in the journey to bring Bella home. We sat on the questionable carpet one more time and looked into her eyes. We both spoke to her directly, hoping that she would get a sense from our matter-of-factness that what was about to happen was just an inconvenient way to get her safely home to her forever life. She looked back and forth at us both as we spoke, and I desperately wanted to fast-forward the ten or so hours it was going to take for us to get her door-to-door.

I prayed that she would get safely on the plane in Fayetteville, and that everyone that she encountered along the way would be sensitive to her past and to her fear. In our meeting with Beth and Jerry, we found out how common dog fighting is in that region of the country, and I hate to say it, but Brian and I felt incredibly vulnerable in our ability to protect Bella, especially once her care was beyond our control at the airport. Our response to that sense of vulnerability was to regard everyone as suspect.

Brian went down and checked us out, and we made our final descent down the elevator, out the double doors, and to our rented

Impala. Beth had warned us that we might have to help Bella up into the car if we took her for rides. She'd told us that she had probably been transported to auctions with other dogs that she knew were going to be ordered to attack her, and because of that she was leery of car rides. But you guessed it, I got in the back seat while Brian held Bella's leash, and then I called to her. She jumped right in. That should have given us a massive feeling of relief and accomplishment, but it made the pit in my stomach that much bigger.

Why hadn't we just sucked it up and driven home with her? We could have had two-and-a-half days of solid bonding with her, and that probably would have made the introductions with Foster and Jane go much more smoothly as well. But no, instead we had taken the easiest and cheapest route we could, and now this sweet, precious girl, who obviously had gained some trust in us in the short time we'd had her, was going to be thrown on a plane. She'd be at the mercy of strangers who would never understand what she'd lived through or how long we'd waited to bring her home.

17

thanksgiving 2010

We made the short ride to the airport, and Brian dropped Bella and I and all of our belongings off near the entrance while he went to return the car. It was surprisingly cold to me for being that far south, so Bella and I walked up and down the parking lot to stay warm. Again, I tried to look deep into her eyes and assure her that the next few hours were just a hiccup in what was going to be the rest of her life. In my heart I knew that these people were professionals. Getting things where they needed to go was what they did every day; but for some reason, that didn't help me one bit.

After dealing with the car, Brian went in to tell them that we had Bella and found out where we needed to go to drop her off. He let them know our final destination of Minneapolis and asked if it was going to be an issue for Bella to fly all the way through. Brian said the two men he was talking to just looked confused and said that no, she'd be fine. They explained to him what would happen to her in the layover in Atlanta, that we could check in with the flight crew and they would make sure Bella had made it on board before taking off. Everything would be fine. They didn't say anything about the weather, so neither did Brian. We didn't want our dog to freeze, but we did just want to get her safely home.

He came out to join us and before we knew it, it was time. We had gotten all kinds of suggestions as to what to give Bella to sedate her for the flight, but this was a delicate situation as well. We wanted her to be as comfortable and relaxed as she could be on the flights, but there was also the issue of meeting Foster and Jane when we finally made it home. We didn't want her feeling drugged and more defenseless, so we opted instead to give her a small dose of Benadryl which would help her doze off and on, but which should wear off by the time we reached Minneapolis.

We had gotten the kennel ready the night before in the hotel room. Tiny plastic screws were placed, and then, at the advice of one of Bella's fans, we also secured some bungee cords to the crate. In the event of turbulence, our potentially inadequate assembly job would still protect Bella from being loose in cargo. We had loaded the kennel with blankets, toys, treats, and the shirts that we had slept in the night before to keep our scents near her and to hopefully provide her with a little comfort for the arduous journey she had ahead of her. We kissed her and held her tight and assured her one last time that once she got through this last bump in the road, her tummy and her heart would always be full.

We opened the door and Bella let us know in no uncertain terms that she did not wish to go anywhere near the kennel. That was Stage One of the heartbreak that this trip would bring. We ended up having to kind of shove her to get her inside, and I don't need to explain to you the guilt we had with that. She turned around and looked at us, her eyes huge and frightened. We spoke to her for another minute or so and tried to provide the same reassurances. She wasn't buying it. We lifted her kennel onto a cart and brought her into the loading area of the airport—this was it.

They ran her kennel through security and determined we hadn't concealed any contraband; Bella was safe to fly. She was also officially out of our hands until we were reunited in Minnesota. We watched her kennel make her way down the conveyer belt, and we heard Bella's voice for the first time since we had met her the day before. We heard her soft cries as she got farther away from us. Stage Two of the heartbreak began. I remember my eyes burning as I watched a man lift her kennel at the end of the belt and place it on a large cart that would eventually transport her to the plane. He stood and stared at her, and I can't even imagine what was going through her head. She looked terrified.

I wanted to scream at him and tell him she was afraid. Couldn't he see that? Did he have a soul at all, or did he enjoy intimidating someone who was powerless and afraid? Brian told me not to say anything. He assured me the guy probably didn't see dogs transported that often, that there was nothing he could do to hurt her, and if we caused any trouble, that would be even more of an incentive to not take the best care of Bella that they could. And of course he was right, so I remained silent and made a mute promise to Bella that this would be the worst thing we would ever do to her.

As I've said, Fayetteville is a tiny airport, and there are windows everywhere, so we could see Bella's kennel in a holding area from the gate where we would take off. We watched as it finally made its way onto a mobile cart that was driven to the plane. We watched as her kennel made it up a second conveyer belt into the cargo area of the plane. And we watched as one of the men with whom Brian had spoken earlier gave us a thumbs-up when he saw us watching from the gate.

She had made it onto the plane, and we both felt a little better. A little, not a lot. I really hoped that the Benadryl had started to kick in. The flight to Atlanta was uneventful for us, and I prayed that it was for Bella as well. Brian reassured me over and over that she was fine, that it was probably dark down in cargo, and that the hum of the plane was helping her sleep. He was so good at staying calm when I know he was feeling anxious as well. I appreciated him immensely that day.

We landed, and they must have been doing loads of construction at Hartsfield-Jackson because it seemed like they let us off right on the runway. We were being hustled inside but not before I could see her kennel coming down the belt. I desperately asked the woman who appeared to be in charge of this circus if I could just go peek at her and make sure she was OK. I got a "no." Not a very nice one, either.

We wound our way inside and made our way to the bar. I don't know about you, but generally speaking, airport bars are among my favorite places on the planet. It's as if time doesn't exist there. Not even in Vegas is it as socially acceptable to suck down cocktails in the wee hours of the morning as it is in an airport bar. We ordered some breakfast and a Bloody Mary and speculated on how Bella was doing. We had a two-hour layover and couldn't imagine what she thought was happening to her. Hopefully, wherever she was being housed until our next flight was reasonably quiet, but knowing the size of the Atlanta airport, we doubted this was the case. Our breakfast came and we both picked at it, but I don't think either one of us felt particularly hungry. We called family and wished them a happy Thanksgiving, and finally it was time to board.

We made it onto the plane and accosted the first flight attendant we found. "Our dog is supposed to be on board and we were told that someone from the flight crew would verify that before we take off and we just want to make sure that you guys are aware and when will we know that she's here?" Luckily, the woman that we spoke to was much calmer than we were. She knew all about Bella, and we wouldn't take off until the pilot had received verification that Bella was on board. OK, this was the home stretch and hearing that finally made us both feel better.

We took our seats and craned our necks, watching and waiting for someone to come and tell us the news we wanted to hear. Pretty soon, that same attendant came walking over to us with a big smile on her face. "The pilot just received verification that your dog is board. Her kennel is in bin C-4." That meant nothing to us, but we thanked her profusely and sat back. The news that Bella was on board had done way more to relax us than the Bloody Mary had. This was it; Bella was three-and-a-half hours away from home.

As with the previous flight, this flight had very little drama involved. We sat back and watched out our window as the sky got darker and darker at 29,000 feet. We could almost feel the air getting colder and hoped that the climate-controlled cargo area was keeping our Bella safe and comfortable. I can't remember how many times the "fasten seatbelt" sign came on, but it wasn't many; things were smooth. Brian and I tolerated that flight better than anything else we had experienced that day. Regardless of how miserable Bella was, how scared she was, or how convinced she was that she was being thrust back into the devastating life that she'd endured for who-knows-how-long, we knew that she was safe, and that she was getting closer and closer to the time when she would be back in our care.

We would do our best to make right all the wrongs that had happened to her that day, that life. We would get her home, and it would be like the safety of that crappy hotel room in Fayetteville, only way, way better. We felt the sensation in our ears before we heard the announcement; they started to pop, just a little. And then we heard, "Ladies and gentlemen, we have begun our initial descent into the twin cities of Minneapolis and St. Paul..."

I hated every single person on that plane. I'm not proud, but it's true. I think that God assembled an army of the slowest people from around the planet just to make our last minutes before we got to Bella that much more agonizing. It appeared that everyone brought their biggest, most bulky carry-ons, along with their man purses, laptops, pocket dogs, and at least seven of their favorite periodicals. I even saw a couple meticulously checking their pockets to make sure they didn't get off the plane without the inflight peanuts they were too cheap to throw out. Hey, they paid for the ticket; they may as well reap what few perks that gave them. At last, we made the slow and steady march off of the plane. Bella, here we come, I thought.

The temperature difference between North Carolina and Minnesota was obvious, and we hoped that Bella hadn't gone into shock between the plane and the airport. We were told that large cargo could be picked up at Gate 9, so Brian made his way there, and I went to pick up our luggage. At the risk of sounding trite, my heart was in my throat. It was go-time. Bella, the dog that we had found on Facebook, whose story had broken our hearts and whose face we loved before we ever saw it in person, was in this airport. And unbeknownst to her, she was about to make her way to our little one-and-a-half story in Northeast Minneapolis. There, Foster and Jane had no idea they were waiting for their new big/little sister. That would happen soon enough; I couldn't be worried about the introductions just yet. Because Bella, the dog we found on Facebook, was in this airport. And she was coming home.

I picked up our suitcases and raced to get to Brian at Gate 9. I fully expected him to be standing there beaming at me with Bella's huge kennel beside him. As I approached, though, I could tell he was worried. He was leaning up against the wall, shooting glances at a huge door through which it appeared Bella would be coming any minute. There was a huge line to talk to a cargo agent, but Brian said he already spoken with someone, and they had told him that when Bella was ready, someone would bring her out. We'd probably been off the plane for about twenty minutes at this point, and neither one of us had any idea how long it took a crew to get a dog from the cargo area to us at Gate 9. We reassured ourselves that they had confirmed that Bella made it onto the plane in Atlanta, so now it was just a matter of being patient while she made her way to us.

Another twenty minutes or so passed, and Brian had again stood in the line to inquire about Bella. He got the same answer. When he asked how long the whole process usually took, he got the garden variety "every scenario is different" answer. Finally, a man in a gray work jacket came hurrying over to us.

"Are you waiting for the dog coming from Atlanta?"

"Yes..."

"It's one gate over. It's been there about ten minutes or so." You've got to be shitting me.

We grabbed our suitcases and hustled—and I mean hustled—one gate over, and sure enough, there she was. We called out to her as we ran up to her kennel and bent down to look her directly in her eyes when we finally got there. Not surprisingly, she looked absolutely terrified. She wouldn't focus on us; rather, she had sort of an absent, faraway look in her eyes. She appeared to be looking around us rather than at us, so rather than spend a ton of time trying to comfort her, we found a cart, loaded her kennel onto it, and made our way to the car. We'd have all weekend to apologize for the last twelve hours.

We got to the ramp where we'd parked our car the day before, and Brian went to find it. He'd pull up in front of the double doors so that Bella and I could hop in. My job while he did that was to take Bella out of her kennel, secure her leash, and break the kennel down so that we could fit it in the trunk. I'd put myself through the drill on a few different occasions just to prepare for today, so I was pretty proficient at it. I kind of wished someone would have been there to watch; they probably would have been impressed.

I got the kennel ready and took it and Bella to the set of double doors. Bella still looked overwhelmed—the same as I felt—but I was sure that once we got her into the car, we'd both start to settle down. And we did. When Brian pulled up, we used the same routine that we had in Fayetteville. I sat in back while Brian held her leash. I called her, and much to our relief, this time, like last, she jumped in without hesitation. We were elated. The air was as cold and crisp as I'm sure any that Bella had ever felt. Brian weaved our way out of the airport ramp, and we drove into the dark blue night, making our way toward our new lives together.

As with the rest of the "getting Bella" experience, her introductions to Foster and Jane had been very carefully planned out. This didn't mean there was no room for error, or that we felt completely confident about how smoothly things would go, but we felt the strategy we had come up with was as fool-proof as it could be. We would get home, and I would walk Bella around the back yard to get her used to the smells, possibly giving her a signal that new dogs were in her not-so-distant future. Brian would say his hellos to Foster and Jane and then sneak them out the front door for a nice, long walk. Hopefully, that would get some of their excitement and energy out of them. Once they were gone, Bella and I would go inside, and she could have free reign of the place. I had no idea how adventurous she'd be on her initial trip inside, but at least she could acquaint herself a little with the scents and sights of her new surroundings.

Well, the first glitch came as we pulled into our alley and came to a stop. I jumped out and called to Bella, gently giving her leash a tug. Bella came to the edge of the backseat and abruptly stopped. There was snow on the ground, and we could tell already that Bella didn't like snow; she was not coming out of the car. This was one problem that we hadn't planned for. I tried my happy voice and my kind-of-but-not-really stern voice. I tried a treat that I had in my pocket. I patted my legs and brought some snow to her face to show her it wasn't as scary as it seemed. Well, apparently it was as scary as it seemed because Bella retreated backwards and gave me an "I guess I came all this way to live in your car" look. So Brian got out of the driver's seat, and for one last time lifted Bella up and out of the car and onto her first Minnesota snow.

One thing that I remember so well from that first night is how Bella would shake and shake despite wearing her pretty purple jacket. Because she was a Southern Belle, we figured buying a warm winter jacket was appropriate, so we found one that matched her leash and collar. We had put it on her before she was loaded in Fayetteville, but as we made our way around the back yard, she would alternate between sniffing and pausing to give herself a good head-to-tail-shake. It was as though she was trying to shake off the cold. It was adorable, but I felt bad that she had at least four more months of the bone-chilling temperatures to endure. But she was here. I couldn't believe that Bella was finally here.

Brian called and said that he, Foster and Jane were out of the house, so Bella and I made our way in. I took her leash off when we came in the door, stepped back, and tried to gauge her reaction. You could tell that she was on a heightened sense of alert. She walked in a crouch and her eyes were huge. Her nose was going overtime as she made her way around the kitchen. She regularly looked back to see where I was, and I didn't know if it was because she perceived me as safety or a threat. She made her way into the living room, the bathroom, the office, and finally the guest room. I stayed about five feet away from her the whole time. She seemed OK—not perfect—but definitely OK.

Brian called again and asked if we were ready to start the intros. "Well, I guess we have to be." I didn't know how else to answer.

Bella and I went into the living room and I sat down beside her. I looked at her and tried to sound as soothing as I could while I told her that she was about to meet her brother and sister. I told her that we love them very much, just as much as we love her. I explained that these would be the dogs that would show her that all dogs just want to snuggle, snooze, and wrestle—not hurt her or each other. They were going to show her what it was like to once and for all have a pack that was all hers and would be forever. And then I heard Brian come in with Foster.

Brian left Foster's leash on and led him into the living room. Dogs are smart. Whether he could smell her, could sense from Brian's demeanor that something was going on, or whether he used that sixth sense that I firmly believe dogs have, Foster knew that Bella was there. He pulled Brian into the living room like he was on a mission and spotted Bella immediately. He dragged an almost-helpless Brian straight to her and gave her a real once-over. He sniffed her all over: ears, mouth, belly, feet, and tail. She didn't move, and I mean at all. Her eyes were huge, and she didn't necessarily look scared, but she looked like it wouldn't take much more to get some sort of reaction from her. And if we did, what would that reaction be? We pulled Foster off and Bella remained motionless. We tried to take some time to soothe her, but Jane was still outside, and it was cold. Brian went out and put her leash back on. If any dog was going to get a response from Bella, it was going to be Jane.

I heard them come inside and Jane pranced in the living room the way she always did, like she was arriving at her own cotillion. She spotted Bella and charged straight over to her in what I would describe as typical "most popular girl in school seeking out the new girl in that bitchy way only popular girls can" fashion. Bella must have recognized Jane's alpha-ness and she didn't like it; almost immediately we saw Bella's top lip began to rise. We quickly tried to pull Jane back and comfort Bella but it was too late. Bella bared what was left of her teeth and lunged at Jane, not once, but twice.

Brian jumped off the couch and quickly grabbed Bella by a bit of that thick neck roll she has. He swiftly but assertively pushed her head down and gave a low "No." He let her come back up, and that was it.

A little more drama may make for a better story, but that quick, simple correction was enough to tell Bella that fighting was not going to be tolerated in her new home. We kept a very, very close eye on them for the next few days, but that night, after the introductions were done and everyone had settled in and tummies were full, Bella jumped up on the couch and fell asleep. We covered her in a warm, red blanket, and once again, we were soon listening to her snores.

It had been an exhausting twenty-four hours, and if I thought about it, an exhausting three months of planning and execution to finally bring Bella to us. We all fell asleep in the living room that Thanksgiving night. I woke up around one in the morning and looked around the room. Bella was still sleeping, still covered in the same blanket. Foster was on the floor in front of the window, and Brian and Jane were sleeping at the other end of the couch. I stood up and surveyed the scene, thinking that our family of five was now complete.

At the risk of sounding repetitive, the girl who had stolen our hearts first by breaking them was finally home, and she would be ours to spoil rotten for the rest of her life. I couldn't wait to watch her blossom into the dog she was meant to be. What would her personality be like? Was she going to hate Jane forever? I had never even entertained the notion because she looked so sweet in all of her photos, but what if she was aggressive? I sat back down and put my head back, inhaled deeply, and appreciated the serenity of the moment. There was time for worry tomorrow, and the next day and the next. For now, as far as I was concerned, it was still Thanksgiving. And I had so much to be thankful for.

We all finally made it to bed that night at about 2:00 a.m. and slept in until about ten the next morning. Foster and Jane slept together in their room, and Bella bunked with us. We were letting her sleep with us until we felt comfortable that she was acclimated to her new life. When I woke up the next morning, I felt substantial relief. Bella was home and the introductions were done. Now we just needed to get this renovation out of the way and the five of us could take some much needed down time. We only had three days in our house before we made the transfer to our rental so that the renovations could begin. But it was Friday, and Brian had to go back to work for a half-day, so I was going to be alone with the three pups for the next four hours or so.

When Brian had initially told me he had to go into work for a few hours the day after we got back, I tried to bully him into staying home. Then I tried a guilt trip. Neither one were effective. So late that morning, the day after Thanksgiving, he walked out the back door and I heard the lock click into place. I looked around, and six eyes looked back at me like "Now what?" To my relief, no one appeared hell-bent on destruction...yet.

I gave Foster and Jane a good head scratch and then bent down to look into Bella's eyes. Eye contact was difficult for her; she would look at me briefly then quickly avert her gaze. That was OK; we had all the time in the world. I was amazed that just forty-eight hours earlier we'd never laid eyes on her, and I already loved her immensely. The four of us made our way into the living room to watch a little TV and then it was meal time.

We'd practiced meal time the night before, and it had gone surprisingly well. All three meals were prepared, then Foster's was brought into his room, Jane ate in one corner of the kitchen, and Bella ate in the opposite corner. Foster and Jane were very good about not invading each other's space, and Jane was excellent about waiting to get the OK from Brian or me to go in and inspect Foster's dish when he was done with it. Every once in a while she was rewarded with a skipped morsel or two, but generally she just licked an empty bowl. The dogs' Thanksgiving dinners had gone really well, but today I was on my own, so I tried to act confident as I got the meals ready, and then one by one the dogs were served. And much to my surprise, it was fine.

I couldn't believe it; surely there had to be some complications in bringing a former bait dog into a house with two other big dogs, right? But Bella had so far been as mellow and well-behaved as any dog I'd ever met. And I had never been so proud of Foster and Jane. From my research, I knew that dogs went through a honeymoon phase when a new family member was added and that it was possible that the bad behavior wouldn't begin for another few days, but my concern about being left alone with the dogs on the first day was for nothing.

After lunch I took everyone outside to do their thing, get some good sniffs, and in Bella's case, do a little more sightseeing in the daylight. She seemed to enjoy this, but again she would look around constantly to check and see where Foster, Jane, and I were. And again, I had no idea if this was because we brought her comfort or were a perceived threat. Foster and Jane gave her space, though, and she did fine. I called them all and before we went inside, I decided that we might as well start working on the rules of the house.

Even though Jane is the alpha, the dogs are treated in the order that we adopted them. So Foster eats first, goes outside and comes inside first, gets treats first...you get it. Now that we had three, Bella was going to have to learn that even though we love her as much as Foster and Jane, she would be last in the pack for these things. So we spent about ten minutes that day working on their order for coming inside. It was obvious that among other things, Bella was smart. In fact, she seemed to thrive on the rule that was presented to her. We practiced going out and coming in about three or four times, and by the last time her butt gave a proud little wiggle when I said, "OK Bella," announcing it was her turn to come inside. The only issue was the hesitation she had coming through the door. If I held it open in a way that she had to run under my arm, forget it. It didn't matter how cold she was, she wouldn't come inside. If I went outside and held the door open for her, though, she was fine. There were so many things that we had to learn about our newest girl.

That weekend we had to do the final touches to ready the house for our departure. The upper level was going to be gutted and expanded, and the basement was going to be finished with a game and media room. Much like Bella's arrival, we had been anticipating this for months, and we were ready to get it started and finished. All the upstairs furniture had to be crammed into every available space on the main floor. The basement was primarily used for storage, and we'd be losing a lot of that, so we'd done a massive cleaning and clearing of it about a month prior. There was still a shocking amount of what I'll lovingly call "crap" to deal with, though.

When we were finished, the main level and the garage were stocked to the point that I don't think one more box or end table would have fit. We packed the clothes and toiletries that we'd need for the seven to eight weeks that we'd be gone. Then we added the TV, computer, dog paraphernalia, groceries, cooking utensils, plates, and silverware. Of all the dogs, I think Bella handled the commotion the best. Foster and Jane called this place home, and from their perspective, it probably looked like we were destroying it. Bella didn't have much of a frame of reference, so she stayed relatively calm about the whole scenario—until it came time to leave on Sunday night.

18

a nightmare is not a dream

Brian had been making trips to the rental all day on Sunday, and it was about 7:00 p.m. when the five of us loaded the last of our things into our two cars, said good-bye to our house for roughly the next two months, and made our way to our temporary digs. Foster and Jane rode with Brian, and Bella rode with me. Because of her past, we were uncertain how she'd handle being transported with Foster and Jane, so we opted to be safe over sorry.

I got in the car, and I was happily surprised that, when I called her, Bella jumped in after me with just a slight hesitation. I adjusted the mirrors, fastened my seatbelt, checked on Bella, and then made my way out of the alley. I'm a pretty conservative driver by nature, but knowing Bella's probable limitations made me even more so.

She started out in the back seat for the short drive we had, but she quickly made her way to the front passenger seat. Her eyes large and imploring, I could feel her staring at me. When we got to our first stop sign, I took a minute to try and reassure her that she was safe, that this was just another adventure that she was going to take with her new family. She responded by crawling in my lap. I weighed the consequences of a fifty-five-pound dog in my lap, but rationalized that we were going less than a mile and Bella was scared. In the unlikely event that we were pulled over, I was sure the police would understand, right?

Because of my cargo, I drove slower than I normally would, and I could feel Bella start to shiver as she leaned against me. I cranked the heat, but she continued to tremble. My heart broke yet again when I thought about what sinister things Bella had seen after going on rides similar to this. Had she been thrown into a crate, left with nothing but her terror, dreading what was to come at the end of her trip? We came to a stoplight and I hugged her tight.

She was facing the front of the car, just as I was, so I couldn't see what her eyes looked like, but I know. I know that they were huge, fearful, and far-away. I wanted to cry but I didn't. I wanted to do my best and live in the moment, which I hoped was exactly what Bella needed. Even though she was scared, she was safe, and my job was to help her know that.

We turned the corner when the light turned green and soon pulled into the driveway where Brian, Foster, and Jane were waiting for us. Bella was back on alert, much like she had been a few days ago when she entered her new home for the first time. This time was easier, though. She knew snow, she knew us, and she knew Foster and Jane. And just like with our house, it would take her no time at all to get used to this house. The pups sniffed around the huge yard, with Bella obviously being the least adventurous of the three. Then Brian unlocked the back door, and our entourage headed inside.

We began our night in the rental by letting the dogs check out all three levels, but we had decided that the bulk of our living would be done on the main level of the house. The less space we took up, the less there'd be to clean up at the end. We considered the upper level off-limits and used the basement only for the computer and laundry. Bella stayed very close by our side, but she refused to go either upstairs or downstairs, which was fine. Her world could stay as small as she needed it to. We hung up our clothes, set up our TV, unpacked the kitchen, made the bed, and got the dog beds situated.

At about nine that night we settled on the couch for a bit to wind down before it was time for bed. Brian, Jane, Bella, and I somehow fit on the tiny loveseat that the owners had left in the living room. We turned the TV on to I-don't-know-what; Brian grabbed a beer from the fridge and poured me a glass of wine. Soon after we sat down, I felt a soft elbow in my ribs. I looked over at Brian, and he quietly gestured toward Bella, who was sleeping at his left side. She was grunting in her sleep and looked adorable. But things became much less adorable almost immediately.

Her back legs started moving, then her front. Her grunting became high pitched and panicked-sounding. It scared us, and we realized she was smack in the middle of a nightmare. We gently tried to wake her up, and while we did, her leg movements became almost violent. We began to fear that she might be having a seizure. After what seemed like forever but was probably only a few seconds, we were able to wake her up.

She sat looking dazed, and sweet old Foster came over to check on her. He has always had an expressive face, and his concern for her was written all over it. He approached Bella, and for the second time since we'd known her, she bared her "teeth" and lunged at Foster. You could tell immediately that Foster's feelings were hurt. He slunk off into another room and didn't approach her the rest of the night.

We quickly tried to reorient her, and it was obvious she had no intention of hurting Foster. Whatever demons she held deep within had resurfaced and forced her into "fight for my life" mode. While we talked to her, she looked at us with a sad resignation that will live in my heart forever. Bella was sweet. She was sensitive, and she was gentle. How some monster could have done the things that were done to her made me want to hurt them...hurt them in not-so-nice ways.

Brian got Bella resettled, and I took a treat into Foster. Our grumpy old man was surprisingly sensitive. I sat with him for a while, and then Brian came in and gave him a good belly rub as well. Our family of five would have some growing pains, and Brian's and my duty was going to be making those pains as painless as possible.

19

the burrito debacle

I'd be remiss in continuing Bella's story without backtracking a bit to tell you about Burrito, who came into our lives and eventually Bella's on a lovely day at the end of September 2010. Foster, Jane, and I had just come back from our afternoon walk, and I was taking off their leashes when all of a sudden both of them charged to the back gate like they were sent on a mission of doom from the devil himself. I turned and saw a small gray-and-white cat on the other side of the fence that had fluffed himself up to maximum size to try and intimidate Foster and Jane. It didn't work. Foster and Jane barked, growled, and bit at the fence, apparently intent on destroying this poor creature.

I ran to the fence, pried them both off of it, and dragged them inside. Once we were in, I glanced outside, figuring that little kitty was a half mile away by then. He wasn't. He was still on the other side of the fence, his fur smoothed and where it should be. I put the dogs in their room and went out to check on him. He sat and looked at me calmly when I opened the back door. As I walked to the fence, he stood up and arched his back in a relaxed stretch. He didn't have a collar on and had that scruffy "stray cat" look. I opened the back gate and he started leisurely walking down the alley, so I followed him. He stopped after a few yards and allowed me to pet him, even rolling over on his back accepting a tummy rub. I stood up and said, "Do you want to come inside with me?" He squinted up at me in the sunlight so I took that as a "yes."

I brought him inside and down to the basement. The stairs were open and unfinished, and neither Foster nor Jane had ever been brave enough to venture down them, so I knew he'd be safe. I went upstairs, closed the basement door, and let Foster and Jane out of their rooms. I then went back downstairs and let them see me holding this creature that they had wished to destroy only ten minutes before. Neither one showed any trace of aggression. Instead, they looked at that little fuzz ball like it was the most interesting thing they had ever seen. They had both lived with Tyra, so they knew about cats, but it had been a year and a half since we lost Tyra. I wasn't sure how they'd respond, but they were champions. The cat on the other hand...

I secured the cat in the basement and went to Petco to buy the standard cheap litter box, cheap cat bowl, and not-so-cheap cat food. A couple in line ahead of me congratulated me on the new family member, and I explained that I just found him and didn't want him roaming the neighborhood if he was lost. They were nice and said that they hoped the owners were found. Given Brian's almost anaphylactic allergy to cats, I hoped so too.

I got home and got the cat all set up. I put him in his litter box, and he used it immediately. (It always amazes me how they're so natural with that.) I got his food and water dish set up and then just hung out with him for a few minutes. He was a sweetie that I decided to name "Burrito." It was quirky and cute, and I thought it suited him very well. I didn't let Brian know that we had a temporary boarder. Better to let him come home and relax and then spring the unbelievably cute Burrito on him. He couldn't be mad then, right?

We put up "Found Cat" signs around the neighborhood and received a handful of phone calls, but the description the callers gave didn't match Burrito. We brought him to a vet clinic to have him scanned and found that he hadn't been micro-chipped. I scoured the web pages of local shelters, hoping his lovely mug would show up as a missing pet that someone was desperately searching for. I sent an e-mail to Beth at Eagle's Den explaining about Burrito and asking if she knew how Bella was with cats. With Brian's allergies we knew that we wouldn't be able to keep him forever, but so far no one was stepping up and claiming this sweet guy. We decided to get him neutered and up-to-date on his shots, and then the hunt was on for a wonderful new forever home for Burrito.

We used trusted friends to try and find the home that we desperately needed for Burrito. The demand for free cats was definitely down. Days turned into weeks, and finally a woman at work expressed interest in him, and I jumped at the thought of Burrito going to someone that I knew. She could give me updates, text me the inevitable adorable pictures, maybe even bring Burrito over for the occasional visit. Plus, we were now dangerously close to the time we were to bring Bella home, and we were already worried about her introduction into our family. The easier we could make it for her the better.

A couple of my coworkers were concerned about the pending adoption, but I shrugged off their apprehensions. The fellow nurse who would be taking him didn't exactly have a reliable reputation, but she'd always shared her animal loving beliefs with me. Plus, Burrito was an awesome, loving little guy. How could she not fall completely head over heels for him? Plus plus, we were now less than a week away from going to get Bella—Burrito needed a home. Plus plus plus, I couldn't in good conscience continue to listen to Brian wheeze as Burrito climbed into his lap. So on November 22, two days before we left to get Bella, I watched Burrito being driven away to his new home. I had tears in my eyes but felt wonderful knowing that he would be safe, sound, and secure. And maybe he'd even come over for a visit.

Fast forward eight days. We hadn't even made it into December yet, and I got a text from Burrito's new mom saying that it wasn't going to work out. Burrito had broken a Christmas ornament and was sharpening his claws on the rug. Never mind that she had resolutely stated that she would never declaw a cat, which had led me to believe that she understood that cats will sometimes act like cats. So now we had the issue of sneaking Burrito into our rental because the owners were fine with dogs, but not with cats. There was also the problem of re-introducing Burrito to Foster and Jane, and of course, Bella's first meeting with him.

That Wednesday we met in the parking lot at work and did the Burrito exchange. I was furious with her and furious with myself. Had I listened to the reservations of others, I could have found a home that was truly suited for Burrito. I could have avoided uprooting him not once, but twice. Three times if you considered I still had to find him an amazing forever home. And the introductions would have been done all at once for sweet Bella. But no, in my eagerness to get Burrito placed, I'd inconvenienced us all.

The weather was horrible as we made our way home. What should have taken about forty minutes took close to an hour and a half, and I listened to the protests from Burrito the whole time. When we got back to the rental, I took Burrito downstairs before I let the dogs out of their rooms. I got him situated again, and I could tell from the icy reception I got that he didn't remember the nearly seven weeks that he'd spent with us. Or he did remember and he was just that pissed. Out came the litter box, the food and water dishes, and the toys. I spent a bit helping him get comfortable and then went to deal with the pups. Once Brian got home, we could deal with the Burrito/dogs situation together.

Foster and Jane remembered Burrito right away; Burrito, however, must have forgotten life with big dogs because he made his unhappiness very evident to all of us. He puffed up, hissed, and clawed at anything that came near him. We hadn't let Bella see him yet, and that was obviously for the best. We'd give Burrito a few days to calm down, and then we'd slowly do the intros with Bella. I tried to divide my time as evenly as I could between Burrito and the rest of the family. Brian had offered to take shifts with the kitty as well, but his breathing had just started to improve, so I didn't want to jeopardize it by exposing him to cat-dander central.

I posted desperate status updates on Facebook for all my animal-loving friends that Burrito was now back on the market. I called friends and family and asked them to spread the word as well. We talked about taking him to the humane society, but the thought of dropping him off and never knowing what became of him wasn't an option for either Brian or me. Surely someone knew someone that wanted this awesome boy.

When it came time for the Bella/Burrito introduction, the outcome was not at all what we expected—not that I know what we expected. Brian was kind of cradling Bella while they both sat on the couch. This would help her feel secure, while also securing her from jumping off the couch when I brought Burrito up from the basement. When Burrito and I came around the corner for the first time, something in Bella's demeanor changed. Her eyes got huge, but not huge like they got when she was scared. Brian saw it too; there was something there that we just couldn't read. Burrito was starting to get restless in my arms, so we decided that was a decent enough first exposure and made our way back downstairs.

I didn't bother closing the basement door because Foster and Jane had no interest in Burrito, and Bella had still refused to go either upstairs or downstairs. But no sooner did we get back to the basement than I heard footsteps on the stairs behind me, and there she was. Bella was fast approaching Burrito. Burrito jumped up on a chair to escape, and I intercepted Bella before she could get to him. I called to Brian, but he'd gone outside with Foster and Jane. Bella was trying to get to Burrito, and I had no idea why. She pulled and tugged to get away from me, and I kept saying, "No...no, Bella!" This was the most assertive I'd seen Bella yet. She didn't appear to want to harm Burrito, but in all fairness, we'd had her less than a week. We couldn't be sure of her temperament around someone less than one-sixth her size. We continued to struggle and I turned her face toward mine to tell her "No" again. I'll never forget what I saw.

The devastating heartbreak in her eyes shook me to my soul, and I would put my hand over my heart and swear to God that a part of that soul died that night. What in heaven's name, or more appropriately, hell's name had this sweet girl seen in her tortured life? Bella wasn't trying to hurt Burrito. She was trying to protect him. I later called Beth about the experience, and she said that it was likely Bella had seen cats thrown into the pit as well. She was feeling fiercely protective, and if we could show her that we had no intention of harming Burrito, it could act as a trust-building experience for her. That sounded all right, but from that moment, Bella wouldn't let Burrito out of her sight. She was obsessed with him. She wouldn't even go outside to relieve herself. Brian would, as he'd done so often in the past, have to physically lift her to get her to go outside. She would cry and whine the whole time, and in the course of a day, she actually learned to open the back door to get back inside and back to Burrito. It was distressing to watch. Who knows how many people had tried to break not only her body, but her spirit. Who knows what kind of pain her brown-sugar eyes had seen, and all we wanted to do was help her heal. And I felt like we were failing.

Thank God for our extraordinary pet-sitter, Pat. She put the word out to all of her feline-friendly friends, and a wonderful woman named Tina Larson, along with her husband, two dogs, and resident cat stepped up and adopted Burrito just five days after his return to us. Bella returned to her normal self quickly after Burrito's departure, but it proved to be a valuable lesson in showing us that Bella's new life still had many triggers which could catapult her back to the horrors of her past. We would have to learn how to anticipate them. Of course, we figured with time these would improve, but time takes time.

In a happy footnote I'll mention that Burrito is now called "Lucky." He's a happy, healthy boy who loves his family and is treated like a king. I'd like to go on record saying how incredibly grateful we are to Tina and her family for giving Lucky the loving home he's always deserved. I'd also like to go on record saying I have mixed feelings about the name change.

20

i screamed two words

Six days after we brought Bella home, she was scheduled for her first visit from our amazing veterinarian, Dr. Ann Fisher, and her equally incredible vet tech, Michon. We found the two of them after Foster developed a devastating illness in 2009. What started out as suspected arthritis progressed quickly until almost all of Foster's muscle mass had wasted away and his gait looked like we'd given him a pint of whiskey. His walks dwindled from a mile or so down to a lap or two around the front yard. I'd watch from the living room window as Brian patiently helped him up as he fell every step or two.

While we still could, we got him to his vet clinic, and everyone in their practice was stumped. They came across a neurological study which was being done at the U, and they signed us up for it, but Foster had deteriorated to the point that travel for him became impossible. Plus, with all due respect, our previous experience at the U wasn't one either Brian or I was looking to repeat. We pleaded with his vet to come and see Foster at the house—we'd pay them almost anything—but because of their licensing they couldn't. But they did know of someone...

The first time Dr. Fisher saw Foster she was stumped as well. She spent innumerable hours consulting with canine neurologists, and eventually they came up with a rare diagnosis which fit all of his symptoms to a "T," except that it usually occurred in young, small, female dogs. I remember when she called me with the diagnosis. She asked me if I was driving and when I said "yes," she told me to call her when I got home. I knew it was bad, so I pulled over. I begged her to tell me, promising her I was safer driving having heard the news versus speeding home in anticipation. I can't remember everything she told me, but I was sobbing. One of the last things I remember saying was, "So the prognosis is grim?"

Dr. Fisher replied quietly, "The prognosis is grim." We went over treatment options and hung up. I sat in that suburban neighborhood for probably another ten minutes, and then safely navigated my way home.

To make a long story short, steroids again proved to be a miracle medication. Foster started out on a monster dose, and the dose tapered down to a tiny maintenance dose that he still takes today. He's had one relapse, but other than that he's remained symptom-free. It was a best-case scenario, something that we weren't accustomed to when it came to our pets. We've been faithful to Dr. Fisher ever since.

Bella had met Brian's parents and done well. Dr. Fisher and Michon would be her next venture into the world of kind strangers. They came in the back door of the rental on Wednesday morning with all of their gear minus the scale, which was huge and clunky. Given the circumstances, we all decided that lugging that thing in would probably do more damage to Bella's first impression of them than whatever good would come from obtaining her weight.

Even without the scale, Bella was unsure, but I wasn't at all surprised to see how caring and patient they were with Bella that day. They scraped some skin on her belly because they suspected she had a yeast infection covering much of her skin. Given the dreadful condition she'd been in when she'd arrived at Eagle's Den and the extensive amount of ointments they'd had to use to help her heal, a yeast infection wouldn't be surprising.

She also had an ear infection in her left ear, and from what they could tell, it would be something we would deal with for the rest of her life. They both thought that she'd probably had a chronic infection in the ear for years, and because of that the canal had swollen to the point that it was almost closed. They tried to clean the ear out, but Bella cried and wormed her way out of their grasp. They did a few other less intrusive things like listening to her heart and her lungs, and then suckered her with a treat so that they could deliver a quick squirt of antibiotic deep into the ear canal. Her cries were heard throughout the house and sent Foster and Jane running to check on their sister.

They drew some blood work and, in continuing their exam, expressed their concern about her mouth. The way her canines had been filed had left the pulp exposed; an abscess in her mouth was almost inevitable. We'd have to be diligent in monitoring for swelling in her mouth, and once we got the infection cleared in her left ear, it would have to be cleaned religiously to prevent infection from returning. They said to be patient when doing these things because until her trust in us was stronger, things like this weren't going to be easy.

From Bella's blood work we found that she was infected with hookworms and was also heartworm positive. The hookworm was no big deal, a good three-day de-worming for all three dogs; considering the crap that Foster and Jane ate, they probably could have used it anyway. The heartworm was another story. One of the things that Beth said to us before we drove away that day in North Carolina was, "If Bella is heartworm positive, don't let them treat her." I didn't think much about that comment then. I'd seen dogs on Facebook that were heartworm positive, but I didn't know much about it. Unlike the hookworms, however, what we discovered is that heartworm is a very big deal.

Heartworm infections result from mosquito bites, and cases are reported yearly in all 50 states. If a dog is bitten by an infected mosquito, the chances of the dog becoming infected with larvae are almost 100 percent. The symptoms range from zero clinical manifestations to cough, shortness of breath, brief episodes of loss of consciousness, enlargement of the liver, accumulation of abdominal fluid, and abnormal heart sounds. Without treatment, the infection can eventually lead to death. Our next step in determining our course of treatment was to collect two more blood samples to test for the presence of microfilaria. (Google this if you want to. I could try and explain it, but it's doubtful I'd be able to enlighten you.) Luckily both tests came back negative for the little critters, and according to Dr. Fisher, this was a good thing. Another big positive was that Bella seemed to be asymptomatic. So then it came to discussing her treatment options.

We learned that heartworm can be very difficult—sometimes fatal—to treat. One method was a "slow kill" method. This involved simply giving Bella a heartworm-prevention pill every month (same as you probably give your dog and exactly what we already did for Foster and Jane). This would kill off any new baby worms each month, and the adults would simply live out their life span and gradually die off, resulting in a blissfully heartworm-free Bella. The second option was not as kind. It's called "hard kill" or adulticide.

With the "hard kill" method, an arsenical compound is injected into the muscle of the dog, resulting in the death of all heartworms, including the adults. Something called pulmonary thromboembolism occurs when the parasitic worms begin to block the major arteries of the heart as they die. Sadly, this can lead to rapid heart failure and, eventually, multi-organ failure. Because of this, it's advised to keep your dog completely calm and quiet for at least a month after the treatment is administered. Any increased activity or excitement equals an increased risk of injury or death. Hard kill heartworm treatment was difficult at best for young and otherwise healthy dogs; how would Bella, with her advanced age and life of trauma, cope with the treatment?

Other considerations included the fact that Bella was finally having a puppyhood. One of our favorite things was to go out into the huge yard at the rental and watch Bella. She and Jane had started to play, and every once in a while Bella would start running. She would run and put her face towards the sun and open her mouth in a wide smile. She would breathe in the cold Minnesota air, and as much as she hated the cold, I think there was something about it that she secretly loved. It made me so happy to see her that way that I got tears in my eyes. It was during this time, while we were trying to decide between our options for treatment, that I realized what Beth had meant by, "Don't let them treat her." The hard kill treatment would surely do more harm than good. We talked it over with Dr. Fisher, and she agreed that we should try the slow kill method. If Bella became symptomatic, well, we'd cross that bridge when and if we had to.

I know this may sound like a full plate that we'd served up to ourselves in relation to Bella's condition, and I carefully considered whether or not I should reveal the health issues that she brought home with her after her adoption. I was afraid that people would think that Eagle's Den had given us a lemon of a dog, and I didn't want this to reflect negatively on them. But I believed then, and I still know today that they did the very, very best job that they could for her. Bella was simply a dog with so many issues that it would have been impossible to treat her completely. I consulted Beth about my reservations regarding this information, and her answer to me was not surprising. Beth told me in no uncertain terms that I was to include anything that was the truth and nothing that wasn't.

Brian and I had fallen in love with Bella and were willing to take her as is, a fixer-upper if you will. If we had waited for Beth and Jerry to do everything required to make Bella healthy, we may have never been able to bring her home. Bella has issues that we'll deal with for the rest of her life, and that's because Eagle's Den takes dogs that others would deem hopeless. They invest their hearts, all of their time, and nearly all their own money to the care of these sweet souls.

Beth told me that many people think of rescue as the last step in a dog's journey when actually it's just the first positive step in getting them to their forever life. To quote her directly, "Rescue is nothing more than a bridge to a new life, and I wish more people would realize that." And each dog that gets adopted out who still has issues to deal with will 1) free up space for another deserving soul, and 2) free up veterinary funds that can be used on someone else in need. Each family has their reasons for deciding which dog is right to bring into their lives and their homes, but one thing to consider is how gratifying it is to help a "less than perfect" dog heal. Not just physically, but psychologically as well.

I'll move on, but before I do, I have to say that I love making Foster and Jane happy. To see them nourished, trusting, and loved feeds my soul like nothing else can. That being said, when Bella looks up at me and I see that she knows she's safe, when she is sleeping so soundly that she snores, and when she's so happy to see us that not just her tail but the entire back half of her body wags, well, that feeds both my heart and my soul.

Bella's first winter with us was one of the most brutal that I can remember. Anyone who lives in the upper Midwest has told stories about the winters of our childhoods. The snow and the cold were legendary. Tales of standing on rooftops and jumping into impossibly high snow banks or the tears on your eyelashes nearly freezing your eyes closed are commonplace. Recent winters had been reasonably mild by comparison, but poor Bella's first winter rivaled any that I could remember.

On one of those particularly dark, blustery, winter nights, the five of us were in the back yard. As usual Bella had taken care of everything that needed taking care of and then graciously let herself back in the house, a skill that she'd gotten amazingly adept at. On nights as cold as that one, we usually opted to have Bella and I stay at home, and Brian would walk Foster and Jane. Bella had really grown to love her walks in the short time she'd been with us, but even with her cute purple jacket, we thought the frigid temperatures at night might be too much for our girl who, fewer than three weeks prior, had been living in the balmy South. From her eagerness to get back inside, I'm pretty sure she agreed.

Brian put on Foster and Jane's leashes and they set off. I went back inside with the intention of hanging out with Bella and waiting for the three of them to return. The rental had an incredibly long driveway with a fence that closed near the back edge of the house, thereby enclosing the entire back yard. When Brian walked them at night, he left that gate open to make it easier for them when they returned.

Brian, Foster, and Jane had only been gone a minute or so when Bella began to act strange. She was doing the same high-pitched crying that she did when she was beginning to have a nightmare. I was confused as to why she was doing it, and I bent down to talk to her. When I did, it was like a flip got switched; all of a sudden she was carrying on like a crazy dog. She began barking, jumping, and spinning around. She was also looking me directly in the eye, which in and of itself was unusual. Then she began sort of throwing herself into the back door. For the demure girl that she normally was, she was behaving like she'd lost her mind. The only thing I could come up with was that she was particularly upset that Brian had left without her, so I continued to try to soothe and quiet her.

I have no idea how she did it, but all of a sudden she snaked her way out of my embrace, got both the back door and the screen door open, and sprinted down the snowy back steps. My mind instantly raced to the thought of the gate being open; this gave Bella direct access to the busy street on which our rental was located. I leapt up and ran after her, my socks immediately soaked and freezing as I stepped onto the snow. I could feel my heartbeat down to the soles of my feet as I slipped and fell on the last step. I screamed Bella's name as I slid sideways, hitting the right side of my back on the handrail and eventually landing face-first in two feet of snow at the base of the stairs. It seemed like it took hours to scramble to my feet, an effort made worse after I cut the bottom of my foot on a sharp piece of ice at the edge of the sidewalk.

With my mind reeling, I finally I made my way toward the corner of the house. Please God, don't let anything happen to her. We'd just brought her home; the thought of losing her already made me want to die myself. And how would I explain this to Eagle's Den? They had trusted that we would give Bella the best possible home we could, and now we had exposed her to a danger that we had never anticipated.

I rounded the corner of the house and saw she was about halfway down the driveway. An incredible number of thoughts and fears raced through my head as I inhaled deeply. When I exhaled, I screamed louder than I'd ever screamed in my life. I screamed two words, and Bella must have heard my desperation because she stopped and turned back toward me. I called to her and patted my legs furiously to get her to come back to me. And, thank God, she did start running back toward me, but not before I saw exactly what had caused the last few moments to go into a tailspin.

Somehow, standing in that kitchen, Bella had sensed that a dog was off leash and had run up to Brian, Foster, and Jane. Brian was restraining Foster and Jane from this medium-sized dog that couldn't have done any real damage, but Bella either didn't know that, or Bella didn't care. As far as she was concerned her family was in trouble, and she was hell-bent on helping them. I grabbed her by the collar when she reached me and got her behind the fence. She turned back toward the now-closed gate and started barking furiously at the dog, oblivious to the stress she'd put on me over the course of the last two minutes or so. I dropped to my knees and hugged her so tightly that I think it confused her; she stopped barking for a couple of seconds and just looked at me. Then she remembered the task at hand and became a raving lunatic again. I stood up and pulled her back into the house.

Once we were back in the warm house, I realized just how much my feet hurt. I pulled off my soaking wet and remarkably heavy socks and was surprised to see the lovely shade of light blue my toes had become. There was also a very unimpressive cut on the bottom of my foot from the ice. It didn't look like much, but given its location, it hurt like crazy.

Bella didn't calm down completely until her family got home. Brian, Foster, and Jane were fine. The dog's owner came to retrieve the dog and there was no damage on anybody's end. Thank God again. They returned home maybe ten minutes or so after Bella and I went back inside. By then, my toes were bright red as they recovered from their brief bout of hypothermia.

I filled Brian in on the whole saga, and he was just as amazed as I had been. How did Bella know that her new family was in "trouble"? How could she tell how important it was to come back to me? And how the hell did she get herself through not one but two doors? I'll never forget that night: the pain that I felt at the thought of losing her, the respect and awe that I felt for her loyalty and bravery, and the relief that I felt when she was safely back in the house and out of harm's way.

But it showed us yet again that there was something different and very special about this dog. It re-illustrated how blessed we felt to have her in our lives, and how a very important part of our lives would be making sure she was as happy, healthy, and SAFE as she could be. Oh yeah, and on that note, not only are our gates closed, they're padlocked.

21

that dog is wearing diapers

I woke up one Saturday morning on the typical last two inches of bed I was left with after Brian and Bella got comfortable during the night. I slid them both over a bit, then sat up and stretched. I looked down at what I thought was a little dirt spot on our white comforter, but as my eyes adjusted to the dim light, I saw there were spots all over the comforter, probably fifteen of them. And they weren't brown; they were red. I woke Brian up and, after careful inspection, we determined that neither one of us was dying. This, however, left us with an almost more horrific realization—Bella was in heat.

I had never had a pet that wasn't neutered or spayed before. I had Sadie and Tyra spayed when they were kittens, and rescue dogs and cats are typically spayed and neutered before their adoptions. Because of the timing of the birth of her pups, it wasn't safe to spay Bella while she was still at Eagle's Den, and we had decided that we wanted to wait and give Bella time to adjust to her new life before subjecting her to the surgery. Ideally, we wanted to wait until we were home and settled in before calling Dr. Fisher and making the appointment.

Our reward for our thoughtfulness was three-and-a-half weeks of putting doggie diapers on her, only to have her wiggle out of them six to seven minutes later. Houdini had nothing on this dog. Beth thought that stage of her cycle was lasting so long because of her age and the number of litters she had produced. I thought God was paying me back for something. I won't even discuss Foster, but trust me when I say that it doesn't matter if they're neutered. If a female is in heat, a male dog knows it.

Bella continued her heat the rest of our time in the rental and a few drops of blood got onto the carpet, which was so filthy that after cleaning up after Bella, I realized that it was a lovely shade of beige, not brownish-gray as we had thought. Enough was enough. We appreciated our time in the rental, but it was time to go home. In total we were there almost two full months. It was wonderful to have a roof over our heads during that time, but there is truly nothing like home. One thing that still resonates with us even though we've been home for more than a year is how awful it is to feel like a stranger. Obviously the rental wasn't home. And the daily visits we'd make to our actual home didn't comfort us.

Every level of our house was completely trashed; it's not possible to open up a house without making it look like a war zone for a while. At one point, the designer that helped us with some of our decisions was taking us around, trying to find a space to spread out some samples she had brought. The place was such a mess that we ended up looking at the samples in her car with the heat blasting—and we could still see our breath. They assured us, though, that everything would be fine and eventually it was.

When we arrived back home following the renovations, everything was beautiful. It took them another month or so to get everything sorted out, but we were home. And Bella was still in heat, which made me and our two levels of brand-new flooring very nervous. I think I went through two full bottles of that pet oxygen stuff. Our contractor came over at one point, and I heard him snicker to his partner, saying, "That dog is wearing diapers." All I could reply was, "We should all consider ourselves lucky."

We had to spay Bella sooner than Dr. Fisher wanted to because of her shortened cycle. But when the good doctor thought it was as safe as it could be, we made the appointment and Brian dropped her off that morning. I kept my phone close by so that I could see when Brian called. When I finally talked to him, he sounded exhausted.

Bella had been terrified and wouldn't go in the clinic; once again Brian had to lift and carry her inside. And forget about getting her back to the exam room—she pulled and tugged until she finally wormed her way out of her collar and made a beeline for the front door. The staff and Brian corralled her as gently and unthreateningly as possible, and Dr. Fisher and Michon made their way from the back to sit on the floor with Bella to try and alleviate some of her fear. Nope, that didn't work either. After a good fifteen minutes or so, it became obvious that Bella wasn't going anywhere that Brian wasn't, so Dr. Fisher suggested that Brian walk back with them, get her settled, and then he could leave.

The whole incident left him mortified; his voice was riddled with guilt over walking out and leaving her there. I listened to him describe how terrified her eyes looked as she watched him walk out of the room. It was easier for me to be objective because I wasn't present for the whole ordeal, but even I felt almost ashamed because we had promised Bella a lifetime of love, care, and safety, and now she was in an unfamiliar setting that no doubt smelled of other dogs and who knows what else. We knew she was safe, but Bella didn't. I assured Brian that she was fine and told him I'd call when I had news from Dr. Fisher. We hung up and I was so grateful to be married to a man who was not only willing to take our eight-year-old dog in for her surgery; he was willing to fly halfway across the country to get her, and then fall head over heels in love with her. The Brains really does have a heart.

About four hours later I heard from Dr. Fisher. The surgery took longer than they expected because Bella's blood vessels were all still dilated and engorged; there was more bleeding with this surgery than with any she could remember. But she had gotten everything cauterized and the surgery had gone well, all things considered. They'd also given her a good nail trim and done a more thorough inspection of her mouth.

In addition to what we knew about her front teeth, they also found that her back teeth were ground down, some almost to the gum line. Dr. Fisher thought this was probably from chewing on the bars of a cage or rocks. Bella had been eating a combination of dry and soft food, and I asked Dr. Fisher if she thought this was sufficient. We were more than happy to give her soft food if that was better, but she thought the combination was best; the dry food would help what was left of her teeth. Plus, Bella was a resilient girl who had been through so much; a little dry food wasn't going to slow her down. I thanked her profusely and hung up to call Brian.

From the way he answered the phone I could tell how anxious he was for news. When I told him that all was well and Bella was just starting to wake up from the anesthesia, the relief in his voice was overwhelming. Even when you know the likelihood of something going wrong is minimal, when it's someone you love and want to protect, there's nothing like getting that phone call saying that everything is OK. Bella would be ready to pick up after four o'clock, so I finished work and made my way to get her.

Bella was groggy and still feeling some of the effects of the medicine when I got there. Her gait was off and her eyes were glassy. I could tell she was very happy to see me, though not as happy as I was to see her. I paid the bill then I walked and Bella stumbled to the car. I opened the door to the back seat, but Bella had no interest. We walked around the car, and I opened up the passenger's door. Sure enough, she climbed right in.

When I got in the driver's seat beside her, Bella looked at me with those loopy eyes and reached over and touched me with just one paw. Before I started the car, I took a minute to kiss her little forehead crease, pet her, and assure her that she was going back home. As I did, she put another paw in my lap. No sooner were we driving than Bella weaseled her way onto my lap. "Well," I thought to myself, "this isn't the first time we've tried this." I would again have to rely on the kindness and/ or sense of humor of law enforcement should we get pulled over.

Bella was adorable when we got home. She was either too uncomfortable to lie down or just didn't feel secure enough to fall asleep, so she sat on her bed and tried her hardest to stay awake. The enormity of the day, along with the medications that were now working their way out of her system, was getting the best of her, though, and despite her attempts to fend off sleep, she began to doze off. Slowly her head would start to droop. Then her body would sway just a little, then just a little more until she began to tip over, which startled her enough to wake her up, and the whole cycle would begin again. I'll bet we watched her do that for over two hours. We used treats, toys, and encouragement to try and get her to lie down until finally she succumbed to her exhaustion. She gingerly positioned herself on the bed and dove head-on into a much-deserved nap.

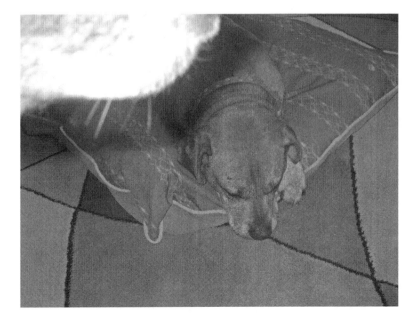

Foster's concern for her was written all over his face, and he continually walked over to give her the once-over to make sure she was OK. I was worried in her vulnerable state she may lash out at him again, but she was simply too pooped. Again we listened happily as Bella's snores filled the room. Her surgery was over and she had done well. She knew that we had come back for her and that she was safely home on her bed. Things that were normal milestones for most dogs were enormous milestones for Bella. Heck, they were enormous milestones for us as well. But feeling her trust for us growing, seeing some of her fears beginning to subside, and hoping that we were replacing at least some of those horrid memories with happy ones were some of the most gratifying things I've experienced. Bella was thriving and turning into the dog she was always meant to be. And that dog was really incredible.

We had been home a little over two months. Bella had healed from her surgery and was back to being a constant playmate for Jane. She had little if any interest in playing with Foster, and we didn't know if it was because of his gender or his general disposition. Jane, however, still loved to play with Foster, and that's exactly what they were doing one night while Brian and I sat on the floor of our newly completed lower level.

All three dogs joined us, and soon Foster and Jane were enjoying a pretty good tussle. Jane is somewhat vocal when she plays, but Foster is excessively so. He barks, snarls, and growls, and if we didn't know him, it'd be next-to-impossible to discern that he was playing and not genuinely ticked off. He and Jane were having a ball, so Brian and I leaned against the wall and had a good laugh watching them. All of a sudden I heard a firm "All done!" from Brian. We use this phrase to let the dogs know play time is over, and they're usually pretty good about listening. As they wound down their play session, I looked over and saw why Brian brought it to a halt.

Bella was gone again. There was the startling vacancy in her eyes that we had seen before, and we quickly realized what had happened. There was no furniture on that level, so every sound echoed. She heard dogs barking and she heard people laughing; she was back in the pit. We quickly surrounded her and tried to reorient her. We used our touch and our voices to try and soothe her, but we couldn't get her back. She began circling the floor in front of us and eventually vomited. We assured her she was safe, we were sorry, and that everything was OK. She slowly began to get the life back in her eyes but not before she vomited one more time.

We had just forced her to face a huge trigger and she lost; we all did. I think Brian and I could have driven ourselves crazy trying to imagine exactly what Bella had lived through. This sweet girl had literally had to stare in the face of hell itself, and we simply had to be more careful about what we subjected her to. Was it fair to tell Foster and Jane that their play dates were over? No, but maybe all puppy scrums would have to be limited to the main level where the sound was more muted. Maybe one of us would hang out with Bella in a different room to try and redirect her from the sounds that brought back the memories of so many of the atrocities that she'd suffered.

Time marched on and Brian's allergies continued to worsen the longer Bella slept snuggled in between us. She'd been with us probably four months by then, and it was apparent that our slumber parties were going to have to draw to a close. I don't think either of us loved the idea, but her nightmares had decreased in frequency. She was also an enormous bed hog. I can't count how many times I was rudely woken up by a head-butt, or if I was occupying more than the two inches of bed that she typically allotted me, she would position herself directly behind me and stretch out all four legs, pushing me over to my designated strip. How a sixty-pound dog was able to man-handle a such-and-such pound woman was completely beyond me, but I'd just lie there while she once again took my spot on the bed that had taken me an hour to warm up just right. Finally, when I woke up one night and heard Brian wheezing beside me, I knew it was time to cut the cord.

We put her brand-new, adorable dog bed in the guest room the first night of our separation. A volunteer at Eagle's Den had given her a pretty pink blanket that she loved, so we put that on top. We brought in a nightlight and changed the light bulb in one of the table lamps so that it now exuded a soft glow. We put an iPod in the room that filtered soft, soothing classical music that we hoped would lull her to sleep. We thought of everything. We gave her a stuffy toy to keep her occupied and copious amounts of kisses to keep the guilt from consuming us. They didn't work.

The door wasn't even closed before Bella began her protests. When we first brought her home, Bella didn't really know how to bark, but lucky for us, Foster and Jane had been more than happy to teach her. What was once a timid little puppy voice that sounded like she needed a lozenge became a full on assault to the senses. Shrill and loud, Bella's barks could be heard throughout the house. Parents who use that "let the baby cry himself to sleep" tactic have my utmost respect. I can't tell you how my heart ached for this poor girl. Forget the lights, the blanket, and the music; none of those things were keeping Bella safe as far as she was concerned. She was safe when she was snuggled with us, and that's exactly where she wanted to be.

Brian and I lay awake and told ourselves that we were doing the right thing and that hopefully this little exercise in independence would be another trust-building experience for her. All of that was fine and good, but listening to her desperate pleas to be freed from her room was horrible. The minutes turned into hours, and ironically, the longer she cried the more we believed we had to make her finish out the night in solitude. We hated it, but if we gave in after a few hours, those hours she spent suffering would have been for nothing. And unless I wanted to slowly kill my husband, Bella wouldn't be able to sleep with us long-term. The sooner she realized that the guest room was safe and warm and would be her own little haven, the better.

I cried off and on that entire night and Brian would reach over and touch my hand. Every once in a while we could hear Jane punch her concrete skull into her bedroom door indicating her disapproval. Ours was not a happy house. Finally, at exactly 4:30 a.m., Bella ran out of energy. We heard one last, sad little whimper and then nothing. She had cried herself to sleep. I think I cried harder after she stopped crying; I felt like we had completely betrayed her. We slept fitfully the rest of that night, and early the next morning we went to let the pack out of their rooms.

Foster and Jane looked at us like, "What the hell did you DO to her?" When I opened the door to Bella's room, it looked like a doggie tornado had hit it. Her adorable, brand-new bed looked untouched. The bed that we have designated for guests, on the other hand...well, let's just say we realized then that Bella was a "nester." The six pillows that reside on the bed had somehow been repositioned in various spots around the bed and on the floor. The comforter and blanket had been pulled down to the middle and that's where Bella had slept.

She was awake when we opened the door and looked at us with tired, sad eyes. We surrounded her, and in typical Bella fashion she recovered quickly. Jane burst in the room to greet her sister, and that was enough to get Bella's backside going. We herded them into the living room, and Bella and Jane had a good little wrestling match before we let them go outside and do their thing. It appeared we hadn't destroyed our dog after all. Subsequent nights weren't quite as painful, and with each she seemed to understand that this was just a new part of her routine. We eventually took out the dog bed; it was obvious that it would never be good enough for her. But if you're ever invited to stay at our house, don't worry—the guest bed has a thorough sanitation regimen that it's subjected to prior to our guests' arrival.

22

the westerfield 22

Spring was beginning and everything was starting to blossom, including Bella. I can't think of any other word to use. Her scars were fading, and her coat was becoming shinier and softer. Her favorite part of the day was every part of the day, but I think she particularly liked the good-morning greetings. We'd let everybody out of their rooms, and two tails and one rottie nub would go crazy. We knew we shouldn't let them misbehave, but they were a jumping and barking mob of craziness and we all loved it, and sweet Bella was always right in the middle of the melee.

New people were still triggers for her, but with each kind guest that came into our home, her trust grew. She was serving as a valuable ambassador for pitties and pit-mixes in general and dog-fighting survivors in particular. No one could believe that her teeth had been pulled, and a handful of people even gave a shocked, "Well will they grow back?!" The horror grew on their faces when we told them no. Bella was our shadow 95 percent of the time, but certain areas were completely off-limits, mainly the bathrooms, closets, and garage. None of these were that surprising, though, and we let her venture as far as her sense of security would allow her.

We posted all of our happy photos and updates on Bella's Facebook page, and our friends and her supporters shared their delight and words of encouragement. Beth was a regular on the Bella page, and I looked forward to her input and advice. We would exchange e-mails as well, but when I looked at my phone one day at work and saw that I had three missed calls from her, something sank in my gut. Beth was incredibly busy, and phone calls were somewhat of a luxury for her during her hectic days; I doubted good news was coming.

I called her as soon as I could, and when she answered, it was obvious she'd been crying. "Have you checked Facebook lately?" she asked me. I said no, and her voice broke again. "Something happened at Westerfield..."

What had happened at Westerfield dealt a blow that spread across the rescue community like a torrid, forceful wind. In the minds of many local animal advocates, the actions of a few had served only to destroy anything that resembled progress in the arena of animal welfare. At Westerfield, dogs had been euthanized in one of the most inhumane ways conceivable.

A volunteer named Diana came forward on a day in early March 2011, concerned about dogs that were missing from their kennels. Diana approached an inmate working at the shelter and was told that animal control officers had taken the dogs across the street; he then told her they had taken the dogs there to shoot them. A horrified Diana, along with members of a local rescue group, made her way to the landfill that the shelter worker was speaking of and began digging. The inmate hadn't lied; in addition to numerous shell casings, the bodies of two dogs were quickly found, both with fatal bullet wounds to the head. The inmate told her that twenty-two dogs had been killed and when word got out about the killings, the public quickly named the lost dogs "The Westerfield 22."

The reaction to the news was swift and strong. Rumors spread that some of the dogs killed actually had rescue commitments in place, and graphic images began circulating that had animal advocates from all over the United States and the world sending their disapproval to the sheriff in charge of the shelter. An investigation was launched, but because the shelter is sheriff-run, the local authorities were essentially investigating themselves. Crowds gathered on the lawn of the state capitol in Columbia to unite their voices in protest. The attorney general and the South Carolina Law Enforcement Division eventually stepped in, and the four animal control officers at the center of the allegations were placed on administrative leave.

Westerfield wasn't a stranger to controversial treatment of their dogs. Accusations of dog-fighting at the shelter were relatively commonplace. One woman told a local news station that she approached a volunteer and asked to see their "game dogs." She claims the volunteer brought her to a section of the kennels filled with pit bulls and even staged an improvised fight to show her how aggressive one of the dogs could be. Almost more shocking are allegations that the volunteer then threw a small, mixed-breed dog into the kennel with the aggressive pit bull. The dog was killed instantly before her eyes.

Local advocates assert that once the investigation was taken over by the South Carolina Law Enforcement Division and the animal control officers in question were placed on leave, sheriff's deputies were tasked with taking over care of the shelter. They say these deputies told a local rescue group that had been active with the shelter for years that their services were no longer needed.

According to some accounts, deputies were not adopting dogs out; rather they were giving them away or selling them for the bargain basement price of one dollar, often times unaltered and without vaccinations. You can imagine the likely fate waiting for these animals in their new "homes." In the end, the punishment for the four animal control officers, whose job it was to protect these animals, was four months paid administrative leave before they were eventually terminated. They had four months to sit at home, visit friends, go on vacation, go to a movie, whatever they pleased, while still cashing a paycheck.

There is one positive element that came out of the tragic ending suffered by the Westerfield 22. Their deaths opened a bright and beautiful door for 150 to 200 other dogs throughout the state. On September 17, 2011, to honor the memory of the Westerfield 22, dogs from several county shelters, including Westerfield, were picked up by a volunteer pilot program and flown to foster families and no-kill shelters around the region. Forty-five pilots selflessly used their own time, energy, and planes to get those dogs to safe environments in Washington DC, New Jersey, Georgia, and Florida.

As an animal lover, this story would have hit close to home regardless. But this was the shelter where Bella started her journey to us. That could have been our Bella that was led across the street, believing she was getting some fresh air and a walk. That could have been our Bella who watched in horror as dogs were gunned down around her. That could have been our Bella who, after everything she had endured, spent her last moments knowing her life was, after all, coming to a violent close. That could have been our Bella's lifeless body callously thrown into a superficial grave. Thank God it wasn't our Bella. But each one of those dogs was somebody's Bella.

23

just a dog

It feels like Bella has been with us forever. I think about our first night in that crappy Fayetteville hotel, Bella surrounded by strangers, being so afraid that her only option was to literally collapse. I think about that faraway look that she doesn't get so often anymore. I think about how much we loved her in the months before we met her, and how the first time we ever heard her voice was when she softly cried while being loaded onto the conveyer belt at the Fayetteville airport. I think about how strong her voice is now and how fearless she has become. And then I have to remember that Bella will always be different, and that different isn't bad, but it does require a little more consideration and care.

There are some parts of Bella's past that she still holds very close, and I was reminded of that one evening recently when I was giving Bella a "standing tummy rub"; she loves them. Well, I got a little carried away, put my arms around her thick barrel chest, and picked her up, just a little; she does weigh sixty pounds after all. I put her down immediately, remembering her response to this action in the past. Lifting her up used to be something that caused her incredible distress. It was one thing that caused Bella's eyes to go to that horrible, vacant place that we hated seeing.

This time, though, she jumped at me, looked me square in the eyes, and pushed her squat little body into my legs. "Huh," I thought to myself, "maybe we've conquered that fear, too!" When Brian came home, I told him what had happened and gently picked her up again while he gauged her reaction. When I did, he told me to put her down and said that her tail had secured itself between her legs the second I had picked her up. When I put her down, she made the same eye/body contact as before, only this time she also vomited, not once or twice, but four times.

A lump grew in my throat when I realized that what I thought was excitement at my attempt at affection was actually Bella reorienting herself to her present. She wasn't being picked up to be tossed in the pit; she was still here with her family, and she was trying to remind herself of that. I was racked with guilt as I had been so often when I failed to adequately care for Bella's emotional scars. There are memories that she'll live with forever, and I'm constantly reminded that despite all the progress this little miracle has made, it will always be our job to keep her in her present.

People still marvel at Bella's story, and if ever there was a dog with star quality, Bella is it. She looks up at our guests with her sweet and cool maple syrup-colored eyes, and they're powerless. If you're not paying enough attention to her (and to Bella it's never enough), she'll put one paw on your arm or your leg, just to remind you that she's there. She will watch when Foster or Jane is getting affection, and to her, I think it's almost as good as getting it herself.

This experience with Bella has convinced me that "pack therapy" is immensely valuable in rehabilitating dogs. We were worried that our two big dogs would be a deal-breaker in being able to adopt Bella, but actually what they did was show her what her role in our family would be. Bella saw the minute we brought her home the kind of love and care that Foster and Jane receive. It helped her to see what our intentions for her were, and I have no doubt that she allowed her trust for us to grow much, much faster than she would have without the presence of her siblings.

Foster and Jane have taught Bella some good things and some not-so-good things, but the best thing they've taught her is that a hand will never be raised against her again. They've taught her that it's OK to be brave, and it's OK to be scared. They've taught her that whenever Mom or Dad drops an expletive in the kitchen, that's your cue to get off the couch and see what they dropped—it might be something good. They've taught her that the best thing in the morning is to race upstairs and throw all sixty pounds of you onto Mom and Dad's bed. Sometimes you land right on top of them, and while it's incredibly uncomfortable for them, for some reason it's really, really satisfying to you. They've taught her that there is a direct correlation between the significance of the consequence for misbehaving and how cute you looked while misbehaving.

This is not to say that Bella is a perfect dog, not by a long stretch. When she and Jane are sharing guard dog duties at the living room window, Bella does have a troubling habit of trying to initiate a fight with Jane. Considering her past, I think she gets caught up in a "fight or flight" moment. We've always been able to verbally separate them, but it's one reason that our dogs will never be left unattended with kids, inexperienced dog people, or other animals.

While I'm on the subject, I'd like to quickly say that no dog should ever be left unattended around these individuals. I always tell people that my trust level for my dogs is approximately 98 percent. They are dogs, so it will never be 100 percent. Every story that you hear of a dog attacking a child is the fault of the adult who should be present and in charge.

Do I ever, in my wildest imagination, think that Jane would ever forgo her incredibly sweet nature and turn on a child? I don't think that's even conceivable. Would I ever leave her alone with my eleven- and fourteen-year-old nephews or my two- and five-year-old nieces? Never. As Jane's guardian it is my job to keep her and everyone else safe. God forbid if anything were to happen, my nephews or nieces would be seriously injured, and Jane would be gone forever. And it would be my fault. OK, so don't trip over my soap box on your way out, but that is an issue that plagues me every time I hear of a dog attack. And don't even get me started about media bias against pit bulls...

It's relatively common for people to praise Brian and me, to tell us what a good job we've done with Bella, that they can't believe the distance we traveled to obtain her, etc. My response to that is always the same. Brian and I have done nothing out of the ordinary. In fact, in all fairness, we're the fortunate ones, not Bella. Yes, we took a chance with her, but it's almost like Karma rewarded our good intentions by giving us the sweetest, wisest, silliest, and loveliest soul I've ever met.

Again, I know I've made this point many times, but we don't love Bella more than Foster and Jane. It's simply impossible not to look at Bella when she's sitting next to you with just one paw resting on your leg and try and imagine what atrocities her beautiful brown eyes have seen, what horrors her ears have heard, and what pain her body and her heart have felt. Despite all that, she wants nothing but to have you look into her eyes, tell her you love her, and kiss her on her little forehead crease. She wants nothing but to snuggle in your lap or play a spirited game of what we call "Crazy Feet," where Bella lies on her back and you play with her feet while exclaiming in a horrible, high-pitched song, "Bell-a's got CRAZY FEET, she's got CRAZY FEET! Bella Bella Bella's got CRAZY FEET!" It's awful. I have no idea how Brian, Foster, and Jane can stand it.

On that same note, I'd like to stress that just as there's nothing truly unique in Brian and me, the same can be said for Bella. Yes, she is wonderful and loving and in general spectacular, but what dog isn't?

In the area where Bella was dumped, there have been twenty-one pit bulls stolen in the last two weeks of this writing. Fortunately, seventeen were recovered when the individuals returned to the scene of the crime to steal more dogs. It's doubtful their intent was to train them as therapy dogs.

The dogs bred to be used in dog fighting are dogs that want you to tell them you love them, kiss them on their forehead creases, and maybe even play a game of Crazy Feet. Instead, they are forced to endure the same hell that Bella did, only most won't make it out alive. They'll die alone and in pain, their hearts empty, having never known a loving touch. Or, they start out in a loving family, only to be stolen and brutalized. An equally troubling development is the "Free to Good Home" trend. Every single dog listed as such on Craigslist and elsewhere is in danger of being adopted into far-less-than-favorable conditions.

In February 2012, a dog was found struggling in the cold waters of a lagoon in Milwaukee, WI. When rescuers got to her, they were stunned by her condition. She bore the scarred and beaten body indicative of a bait dog. It was obvious she had been thrown there by whoever was finished with her. She was suffering from hypothermia and seizures, so animal control workers decided the most humane thing for Lucy was to euthanize her. How do I know her name was Lucy? Because the dog found struggling for her life, the life that she eventually lost, had a microchip. The family was contacted and stated that they had given Lucy away years ago, to what they thought was a "good home." A family that loved their dog enough to microchip her had no idea the ending their precious friend would suffer. Can you imagine anything worse?

Dog fighting is increasing in this country, and while events in the past several years have indeed shed light on the severity of the problem, they certainly haven't eradicated it. Dog fighting is now a felony in all fifty states, but in half of those states, it is only a misdemeanor to attend. One of those states includes the state of Minnesota.

I don't know if Bella had a family prior to ours or not, but it's hard to imagine this amazing girl surviving that life for all of her eight years. If she did have a family, I hope that they loved her, and I hope that any dog they have in the future is safe and protected from evil-doers; there are plenty of them out there. I wish we could tell them that we have Bella and how much we love her. I wish we could thank them for giving her such a loving foundation for us to build on. But all we know for sure is that this is a girl that arrived at Eagle's Den Rescue shortly before Labor Day 2010. Her body was covered in scars; she was emaciated and pregnant. Her journey has involved a tremendous amount of healing, and our part of her journey has changed our lives.

I've learned things I wish weren't true, but now that I know them there's no turning back. I know some of my friends hate that I turn everything into a cause. I know a few that have referred to me as "the one with the dogs." To those who don't have the capacity to unconditionally love someone with more than two legs, all I'll say is I'd rather be crazy like me than crazy like you. Bella has taught me that absolutely anything can be forgiven, but as hard as I try, she'll always be a lot better at that one than me.

One afternoon, Brian and I went to a movie. When we got home, they all greeted us in typical dog fashion as if we'd been gone weeks instead of a couple of hours; reason #658,003 to have a dog: they're good for your self-esteem. As the other two were barking and telling us how great their naps had been, Bella grabbed a stuffy toy and tossed it high in the air. When it landed, she jumped in the air and pounced on it and proceeded to give it a series of death shakes that would have made any dog proud. She ran up and down the hall, and you could feel her joy. That's one thing that strikes me; it's so obvious that Bella feels joy. Not just happiness, but pure, unbridled joy. Beth was right when she said that loving a bait dog is different than loving any other kind of dog; her appreciation for everything is unlike any that I've seen.

As Bella went racing past us with a stuffy in her mouth, I looked at Brian and he was shaking his head. "What are you thinking?" I asked him.

He was quiet for a minute. And then he said, his voice hushed and still, looking at Bella, "She's just a dog. When did she become just a dog?"

I thought about it, and I didn't know, but he was right. Somewhere along the way just enough of the fear, apprehension, and horrific memories had gone away to leave us with just a dog—a sweet, silly, joyous, and loving little survivor that has blessed our lives beyond anything I could have imagined; and I don't want to imagine life without her. Because somewhere along the way Bella got just a family, and together, the five of us are just right.

24

my name is bella

My name is Bella. I know you know that, but having a name again makes me very proud, so I felt like sharing it with you one more time. I can tell I'm a long way from where I started by the way my body feels, in more ways than you think. They say that dogs and cats can tell where they started, and if they're moved, they are able to navigate back to where they're from using nothing more than their internal homing system. I shut that system off. I know I'm a long way from "home."

You're going to think I'm crazy, but one of my favorite things about this place is the cold. The cold reminds me of how far away I am from where I came. Don't get me wrong—it's horrible to walk outside and have the bitter wind take your breath away. But there's nothing like going out in the frigid night, emptying your bladder as fast as you can because you feel like your paw pads are going to freeze right off, and then feeling the warmth of your home before you're even through the back door. The house glows bright, and either Mama or Papa are standing there, holding the door, and smiling at you as you burst through. It's a warmth that you feel that starts on the outside and works its way in.

There are a lot of things that I don't know. I don't know why I ended up here. I don't know why it took me so long to end up here. I don't know what I'm doing differently to be treated so differently, and I don't know what happened, or what is happening to those countless other dogs that I used to share a life with. I hope that they're in a cold place, too, feeling warmth that starts on the outside and works its way in.

There are a lot of things I hope for those dogs. I hope that someone is smiling down on them, filling their tummies full of food and their hearts full of love. I hope that my precious babies, all of them, including the last litter that I ever had, are looking down at me and that they see the wonderful life I'm giving my new family. And I hope they're as proud of me as I know I would have been of them. There are moments that I still think of those sweet pups, and the heartache never goes away. But if those dear babies had to go where I came from, I would rather bear a heart heavy with grief any day. The babies that I had that are still on this earth—every day I imagine you sleeping on blankets in front of warm, soothing fires. I imagine you sniffing flowers and marking your territory in a field that will never be challenged. I hope you know that I love you. I pray that your suffering is over, or better yet, never started.

When I first got here, I was scared to go to sleep. What if I went to sleep on one of those soft, tall beds that I'd always dreamt of and woke up back in my cage, my stomach empty and my own waste burning my feet? I remember dreaming of my family when I was in that cage, and then I would wake up to a reality that I thought was my forever. I still dream about that cage. I dream about the dogs coming at me, their eyes filled with fear and determination—determination to make the men happy and fear for what would happen to them if they didn't. I still dream about those things, but not as much. I remember what it feels like to be kicked, punched, cut, and choked, though I wish I could forget. I know that Foster and Jane know that I'm different from them, but they don't treat me that way anymore.

I've learned a lot from my new family. I've learned that there are rules that I have to live by, and if I break a rule there is a consequence that I don't like. Mama and Papa use a word "No" if I'm doing something they don't approve of. I don't like that word or the way their voices sound when they use it, but what I do like is that I always feel safe. Even when I hear that word that I don't like, I know I won't be hurt; well, maybe my feelings...a little. I've learned that I'm smart and silly and that I love to play. I've learned that watching me play makes my people laugh and I LOVE that! I've learned that when I'm happy, which is almost always, I make a funny grunting sound that Mama says is my version of a purr, whatever that is. I've learned that it's OK to sleep on the couch and mess up the rugs and destroy the stuffy toys that I love so much. I've learned that Foster eats first, Jane eats second, and I eat third, and that's OK. The anticipation for my meal makes it taste that much better. I've learned that stupid things like sitting on command make Mama and Papa really, really happy. I'm capable of so much more, but if they're willing to settle for that, why overexert?

One thing I don't ever want to forget is how sweet Jane's coat smells. Never in my wildest, craziest dreams could I have envisioned ever playing with another dog without them wanting to hurt me. And I can't believe that the queen bee would want to share her space with me, but she does! She will make a little circle before she lies down, and once she does, she lets out a really contented exhale. That's my signal that she wants to nestle, so I plop down right on top of her. And I feel very safe. And I am very safe.

So I guess this is where I'll sign off. If you have a Foster or a Jane or a Bella of your own, now would be a good time to go tell them how much you love them, how you'll never let anything bad happen to them, and how you'll love them forever and ever. Give them a head scratch and a tummy rub from me. And if you can open your home to a dog like me, I promise you the journey will be worth it. If you don't believe me, just ask my family.

My name is Bella...and it's been very nice to meet me.

25

and finally,

I think the term "labor of love" is vastly overused and somewhat ridiculous; that's why I hang my head in shame when I say that this project has been a labor of love. Not many people get the chance to relive the best and worst moments of their lives, and even if no one besides me ever reads this, all the time, tears, and effort invested in it have been worth every second.

This is an ode to Beth and Jerry McDuffie and others like them who go into the world every day with a desire to make it better and do just that—armed with nothing more than the courage to cause change, and the compassionate heart to see what's truly possible. Beth and Jerry, I admire you and I love you. You have set an impossibly high standard that I will never be able attain, but I will never stop trying.

This is for Tracy Caves and Deborah Farhi, two amazing women who work determinedly to help the at-risk dogs in the area where Bella was found. They contribute their time and resources to ensure adequate living conditions for the dogs being housed in shelters. Tracy says that Bella's story is the reason she became passionate about rescue, and whatever the reason is, the rescue community is so lucky to have them both.

For Denise Damanti, who can never say "no" to a stray dog or a request for input. Denise graciously served as my own private critic and assured me that Bella's story was a compelling one that deserved to be told.

This is for Paul and Marti Jones, Katie Yuen, Adri Rebecca Herron, Jessica Rouse Williams, Dustin Bruce, Brandy Rock, Brandy Church, Theresa Michele Lash (aka Tc Lash), Kathy Hunt, and so many more who have helped Bella along the way. I'd first like to say that some of these people weren't directly involved with Bella, but their inclusion on the list shouldn't be a mystery to them. They all work tirelessly to promote animal welfare, and I sleep better knowing people like them exist in the world. I'd also like to say that with the exception of the wonderful Brandy Rock, I've never met any of these people in person. I've never shared a phone call or, in some cases, even an e-mail. But these are people whom I hold in the highest regard. I doubt that our paths will ever cross, but if they do, I'll relish every moment; drinks will be on me.

To Cynthia Houle, who showed me that you don't have to be a "writer" to write. Because of her, I know that when you care enough, the words will flow.

To Sharon Honeycutt, who has proven herself to be not only an amazing editor, but also an amazing woman. I'm honored that she has been a part of Bella's journey...she's made it just a little bit sweeter.

To Kelly Pederson, a friend who has been there, I just didn't realize how much. She took the turmoil of the production phase and didn't just hold my hand, she carried me. It's official Kelly, you rock.

To the countless number of Bellas still waiting for rescue, I sincerely hope and pray that the world gets the chance to do right by you. So many of us love and cherish you despite having never met you. Please know that in the face of the dreadful abuse and neglect you are forced to endure every day, what you truly deserve is a life filled with love, respect, and dignity. You deserve a soft place to lay your head and enough kibble to fill your belly. You deserve someone to whisper their love to you every chance they get. To you sweet souls, whether you are eventually lucky enough to go to your forever home, or forever Home, please know that you were loved; I hope you somehow felt it. And I hope to someday meet you at the Rainbow Bridge.

And finally, this is my love letter to Brian, and to Honey, and Cayenne, and Nietzsche and Oedipus, and Pepper, and Sadie and Tyra, and Foster, Jane, and Bella. And to all the other amazing spirits that God may bless us with in the future. It is an honor to have been able to share a part of my life with you, and in sharing my life, you also share a part of my soul. You have all changed me for the better, and I can't imagine walking through this life without your footprints beside mine. Brian, you'll never know how much it means to me the way you've embraced our journey together. My gratitude to you is felt with every-thing that makes me who I am. So, with a very humble, yet full heart, I say thank you to you all. You have filled me up with love. And you have made each and every day of this life shine as bright as the sun.

About the Author

Cynthia Schlichting was born in rural Iowa, and moved to Minneapolis, Minnesota in 1992. A self-described "underachiever" and idealist, Schlichting waited tables and went door-to-door fundraising for various non-profits during her 20s. A sudden surge of ambition led her to complete her biology degree, and eventually a nursing degree in her mid-30s. She's been a passionate animal advocate since childhood, and shares her life with her husband, Brian Carlson, their German Shepherd-mix Foster, Rottweiler Jane, and Pit Bull-mix Bella. Their pack of five lives in a quiet neighborhood in Minneapolis, MN.

Eagles Den Animal Haven & Rescue
&
Where Hope Lives Humane Society

40% of the proceeds of "As Bright as the Sun" will go into The Bella Fund, named by Beth and Jerry McDuffie. The Bella Fund will help Eagles Den Rescue and Where Hope Lives Humane Society to treat and rehabilitate other dogs who have suffered as bait dogs.

Eagles Den Animal Haven & Rescue

Beth and Jerry McDuffie continue their work at Eagles Den Rescue in rural North Carolina. They champion a cause that is difficult on the best day, taking in animals that are not only hoping for their second chance at a happy life, but also those who are waiting for their first chance. Many of the animals that come into the Den's care have never known a loving touch or a safe environment, and Beth and Jerry carefully and selflessly rehab hundreds of such dogs each year.

Beth's interpretation of Bella's story, while beautiful, is not unique. It is very common for Beth to "speak" for the animals in her care, and a collection of her work titled "A Dog's Tale" is being developed. Additionally, Beth is publishing a book titled "Charity's Journey – A Message from an Angel".

Beth and Jerry are living the life they were born to live, and countless animals can thank them for it. If you would like to help, or are interested in adopting a "Denizen" (an endearing term used to describe all of the sweet souls currently being cared for by Eagles Den,) please visit their Facebook page or www.eaglesdenrescue.org for information on supporting their important work.

Where Hope Lives Humane Society

Where Hope Lives Humane Society is an amazing non-profit organization located in North Carolina near the South Carolina border. Their mission statement is "Helping to create caring compassionate communities committed to change for the animals through awareness, education and volunteering", and they do this every minute of every day, advocating for animals who have suffered horrific abuse and neglect. They find amazing, forever homes for dogs who would otherwise be discarded, and I'm honored to say that Where Hope Lives Humane Society was the first group to give our Bella her first step to finding her way to us. Please visit them on Facebook, "Where Hope Lives Humane Society" for more information on available dogs and other ways that you can help.

Made in the USA
Charleston, SC
29 July 2012